SOCIETY

AND

RELIGION

– A COMMENTARY ON THE
VIEWS OF FIVE SOCIAL
THEORISTS.

LAWRENCE J. McGARRY

THE VILLANOVA UNIVERSITY PRESS

COPYRIGHT © 1989 by Lawrence J. McGarry

The Villanova University Press
Villanova, Pennsylvania   19085

Library of Congress Cataloging-in-Publication Data

McGarry, Lawrence J.
    Society and religion: a commentary on the
views of five social theorists / Lawrence J.
McGarry.
       p. cm.
Includes bibliographical references.
ISBN 0-87723-056-0
1. Religion and sociology--History. I. Title.
BL60.M24 1989   89-35927
306.6--dc20   CIP

DEDICATION

TO MY PARENTS FROM WHOM I FIRST LEARNED
— MY STUDENTS WITH WHOM I CONTINUE —
AND TO VILLANOVA UNIVERSITY FOR BEING
THE PLACE OF LEARNING THAT IT IS.

CONTENTS

Contents

SOCIOLOGY AND RELIGION
Introduction

In two earlier books I explored some of the ideas of the sociologists Charles Horton Cooley and Emile Durkheim; suggesting ways in which I saw them applicable directly or indirectly to contemporary American society.

The aim of this book is to do the same for three other sociologists: Georg Simmel, Pitirim Sorokin and Robert Park. Then, along with Cooley and Durkheim, to apply their ideas to the relationship between society and religion, a relationship that has always been of interest to sociology. (Max Weber, Georg Simmel and Emile Durkheim devoted entire books to the subject; and, it was far from ignored by August Comte, Herbert Spencer, Karl Marx and, more recently, Talcott Parsons and Robert MacIver. Of the ideas we will be exploring only those of Durkheim and Simmel were originally presented as analyses of religion, although Sorokin's were certainly not unrelated to it.) In applying these theorists to the one phenomenon I hope to be able to show a connection between the thinking of all five of them.

Since Cooley and Durkheim were discussed at length in my earlier books Chapter One will be a brief summary of their ideas on society (however, Durkheim's basic idea of religion will be introduced in that chapter because of the strict identification he makes between it and society). This will be followed by a more extensive treatment and application to our society of the ideas of Simmel, Sorokin and Park; and, a discussion of all five as they are related or relatable to religion. The last part of the book will involve sociology as therapy; a look at a common theme running through sociology, psychology, philosophy, theology

1

and physical science; and, a section on further thoughts.

While this is a work in sociology, in the interest of sharing it with as many as are interested in commentaries on current American society, and on the phenomenon of religion, I will avoid the use of the language of sociology.

CHAPTER ONE
A Brief Look at Cooley and Durkheim
Cooley

In 1909 the American sociologist Charles H. Cooley presented a model of three sequential stages of individual human development that, since they are based in our nature as social, tend all human beings toward the practice of positive behavior toward all. As such, a model that very plainly reflects a positive view of human nature. In short, it predicts that with increasing spatial mobility, increasing contact and communications between those of various ethnic backgrounds (decreasing the power of ethnic groupings to promote the restriction of positive relations to "their own") the course of human history will incresingly move us toward the recognition of humanity as "the one people" that it is.

Cooley's three stages are <u>primary needs, primary groups, and primary ideals.</u> Rare is the introductory sociology textbook (in the U.S. at least) that does not include a section on his primary group within which care, concern and kindness prevail. And virtually all these books write of the primary group as represented by the family within which an individual develops her or his social nature and the subsequent networks of family and friends by which it is maintained. This is undeniably important but (putting off for the moment the primary needs) it does not account for his insistence that our social nature orients us toward the extension of care, concern, kindness to all; that is, to the exercise of the primary ideals. For Cooley, since this positive behavior predominates in the initial primary group (which is the <u>only</u> experience of human contact the very young child has) then the child assumes this behavior

3

to be the standard (the ideal) for <u>any</u> human contacts. Consequently, these ideals are directed not only beyond the others in one's initial primary group, but also beyond the members of her or his subsequent primary groups. As <u>standards</u> for behavior they are applicable to all human contacts, direct or indirect. It is in this that his theory has implications for society, even the world, as a whole.

In addition, he implies that these primary ideals are rooted in human nature itself; that with which we are born and our social nature (we're not born social but with a need to be). In several places he refers to primary needs for kindness, care, affection - needs that can be satisfied only in a primary group. Since the development of social nature depends on their being satisfied or met in the initial primary group then Cooley is indicating that we bring these needs to that group experience; that they are rooted in our nature; that we are <u>born with them</u>. Cooley is saying that we are born with a natural need for care and concern that when met in the kindness, the positiveness, of the primary group, tends us to extend kindness to anyone we come in contact with and even those with whom we have no direct contact. In short, that our nature itself tends us toward concern for the well being of all.

A good illustration of the latter is the caring response of so many people to the plight of complete strangers who are victims of natural disasters. (Incidentally, this phenomenon also illustrates the fallacy of the basic premise of many sociobiologists that individuals are concerned only with their close relatives since they are motivated only by an interest in perpetuating their own genes).

Furthermore, he claims that our primary needs are met in our initial primary group, typically in a "<u>fairly</u> satisfactory manner," indicating that virtually all should

4

attain to the stage of primary ideals. Since fairly satisfactory is far from perfect or even very good then a "fairly satisfactory manner" would certainly cover the initial primary group experience of virtually all persons. However, nature and culture (what we learn) can be at odds with one another. A natural orientation always remains an orientation; that is, it "moves us" toward but doesn't force us to comply. As such it can be countermanded if we are taught directly or by example not to care about those beyond "our own" (family and close friends, ethnic group, etc.). However, since this orientation is in our nature, while such countermanding can frustrate it, it cannot remove it from us.

Durkheim

Unlike the other theorists we cannot even begin a discussion of Durkheim's ideas on society without involving religion since as indicated in the introduction he saw the collective feeling of social solidarity (without which the phenomenon society cannot exist) and the sentiment of religion not only related but the very same phenomenon.

On the first page of The Elementary Forms of Religious Life he states that the aim of sociology is to look for and attempt to explain that which is near enough to us (basic to our human condition) to affect our ideas and actions. That which we are to explain is humanity itself, in terms of its essential and permanent characteristics. In short, to explain human nature or the basic human condition itself. To be concerned basically with the extent to which our social nature affects the ideas and behavior of you and me, of all human beings.

5

In order to accomplish this he concentrated on the phenomenon of religion since he saw it as representing both the essential and permanent aspects of the basic human condition. Quite clearly then this was not for him an arbitrary selection, one of a number of social phenomena he may have used. As noted above, for Durkheim religion and society are inseparable; for him religion is the symbolic representation of society. Its rituals are the external expression of the feeling of union experienced in social solidarity. And, as such, it is necessary for the reinforcement and maintenance of that feeling. In short, religion is as much part of the human condition as society itself. It is important to understand this position Durkheim gives to religion in order to grasp more fully what he thinks about human nature. Our nature is social, we have a need to experience the feeling of union, of solidarity with others. It is this need, attracting us toward one another, that accounts for society and, for him, society accounts for the existence of religion. But what religion represents is not simply the level of the feeling of union actually experienced in a society at any given time but as the symbolic representation of that experience it magnifies it to an ideal. Symbols are the meanings consciously or subconsciously applied to things. When subconsciously applied to feelings their meaning can be experienced consciously as unlimited, as full. This is so because the subconscious, the "place" of our feelings, functions beyond the limits, the reach of the conscious. Consider the difference in conscious meaning of each to the other of two persons who have progressed from simple physical attraction to one another to an exchange of declarations of love. The symbol, the meaning of each to the other has changed - at least while they remain in the full flush of their new feelings - to an ideal or a perfection. Doesn't "love is blind" mean blinded to any limits or imperfections? So, if we are social by nature and religion is the symbolic representation of the feeling of societal solidarity, then our nature itself (which definitely includes the subconscious) attracts us toward greater to unlimited feelings of union. Our natural need for the experience of social solidarity, attracting us toward the widest possible horizon in which it presents itself, results in a symbolic image of complete solidarity.

But for Durkheim this fullness of the feeling of union is not purely of mental origin. The subconscious symbol of the feeling of solidarity is always built on the actual experience of it. So if the source of that experience changes it would result in a corresponding shift in the application of the symbol. But historically there has been an ongoing (and more recently accelerating) change in the source of the experience of solidarity. With the expansion, the growth, of societies they necessarily increasingly came into spatial contact with one another. This created the increasing probability for friendship contacts between individuals across their respective societal lines. Such positive relations are themselves experiences of union. The ideal of union expanding toward, as he put it, a wholity seen by the members of the several societies as more vast than their own (1965, p. 493). While not an experience of union with the societies of others, an experience of union with those of other societies; which he refers to as a "new sort" of social experience. In his book Suicide (p. 336), he writes more specifically of (what might suggest) how this would come about.

As societies developed toward greater complexity, from few to greater divisions of labor (what today we call

7

an "age of specialization") their members would come to see their feeling of unity no longer based on cooperation in common tasks but, rather, on only one bond, their common humanity, a bond that is formed on the basis of mutual recognition that "the human personality" possesses "exceptional value." (1951, p. 336) That is, persons attracted toward one another as persons. Not only would this be a new basis for feelings of union within a society but since it involved a bond based on common humanity would open the way for individuals to experience it with individuals of other societies. In doing so it would involve individuals reaching across societal lines in empathy, friendliness, and friendship, breaking the barriers that had restricted their feelings of union to their societies, weakening but not necessarily destroying their identity with their own societies since a feeling of union with members of another society does not involve identifying as a member of their society. But such identifications with those of other societies can be assumed to be accompanied by a less strict identification with one's own society as the only good one.

That spatial contact between societies has been occurring, with increasing acceleration, is recognized by all observers of social history, but this does not mean that they all agree that it results in an increase in feelings of union across the lines of societies. However there is historical evidence of an increase in empathy on virtually a world-wide scale that seems to support Durkheim's thinking. (Later in the chapter on religion we will see evidence of friendliness and friendship resulting from spatial contact.)

Certainly an increase in sensitivity to what happens to others reflects some level of a feeling of union with them.

But isn't increasing sensitivity indicated by the increasing concern for human rights in a growing number of the world's societies? Where today do we find arenas filled with huge crowds cheering displays of such extreme cruelty as at the "games" of the Circus Maximus? Public torture was common in England until the 17th Century; in France until near the end of the 18th Century; Russia, the beginning of the 19th Century; and, wasn't stopped by the papacy until 1816, when it was forbidden in all Catholic countries. Slavery was accepted by a large segment of our population (including in the North) at least until the Civil War; how many of us today (even in our so-called "red neck" areas) would even think, let alone publicly acclaim the virtue of some people owning, buying and selling others? The holocaust must certainly be considered. But even here, the vast majority of Germans claimed no knowledge of it. While highly unlikely that that many were ignorant of that horrible happening, those who knew as well as those who didn't, in their denial, indicated their shame. And shame is clearly an indication of the recognition of guilt.

Here, it seems, is a correspondence with Cooley's idea that the experience in primary group tends, attracts us (as our contact with or knowledge of others increases) toward widening our horizon of union; a fuller, more perfect experience of union realized in the extension of primary ideals.

Like Cooley, Durkheim also makes a direct connection between human nature and the idea or image of an ideal society. Unlike Cooley, he makes no reference to natural needs that are rooted in the individual for, as indicated above, he recognized no nature for humanity beyond social nature. However, they are both in agreement about our need for society, our need to belong, our need to experience the feeling of belonging.

CHAPTER 2
Georg Simmel

Georg Simmel, a German sociologist, in reaction to his experience of living in Berlin around the beginning of the twentieth century wrote ("The Metropolis and Mental Life") of two characteristics of urban life that he saw as extremely negative ones. Although valuing the stimulation and of urban living as more suited to the quality of life than the dullness of rural settings, he saw a real danger in the tendency of urban life toward over-stimulation and over-complexity. (Before proceeding with his reasons for singling out these two characteristics it is important to note that virtually all parts of our society today, due to high spatial and electronic-communication mobility, are characterized by these conditions. This is certainly true of our suburbs which, together with our cities, is home for the great bulk of our population.)

Over-stimulation due to rapid change (constant newness) tends to produce a defense mechanism he called the blase personality. A personality characterized by a lack of concern for others since those possessing it feel they must be concerned almost continually with their own mental survival. The slogan for the blase person is "Don't get involved." Rapid change and constant newness of people, activities, etc. (the pressure of the "pace of the city," that today doesn't stop at the city limits) force one into a pattern of rapid and constant adapting (more precisely constant re-adapting). Adapting to a new situation and new people puts a demand on one's energy; almost continuous readapting seems, in many instances, to place too many such demands. Simmel understands that the human psyche is flexible enough to adapt to new

11

situations, to adjust to changing conditions; he even sees a value to a limited amount of this in that it increases mental alertness. He seems, however, to be seriously doubtful of the notion that there are no limits to our flexibility.

Constant adapting forces individuals to focus attention on what is going on around them. That is, up to a point. A point of being overwhelmed by adapting to so many external changes that for psychic survival the focus is turned inward. It is this reversal that produces the blase personality. The screening out the external by hiding inside one's wounded, anxious, and therefore, confused sense of self. That is, the blase attitude is a defense mechanism that indicates serious doubt concerning one's own worthwhileness.

The problem of over-complexity of life in highly urbanized societies, while distinct from the over-stimulation of rapid change, tends to produce the same result. Over-complexity among other things necessitates extreme specialization of tasks which has two results. One: individuals become progressively aware that they depend entirely on the knowledge of armies of different specialists to provide them with virtually all their needs. This extreme specialization tends to result, for all involved (since all are specialists), in the feeling of being increasingly vulnerable participants in the life of a society. Society in which, as areas of knowledge multiply, as the totality of knowledge increases its members can assimilate only increasingly narrow portions of it. Secondly, they get further and further away from the self-satisfaction of performing whole, creative tasks. For instance the medical profession today is increasingly practiced by those who no longer treat the whole patient (sometimes they are almost as ignorant as the layperson about other medical specialties); cars today are less frequently than formerly repaired by one person who knows enough about all their working parts to do so. And these are only two of the many examples of what is going on. (Quite clearly no one wants to return to simple medicine; but simple cars may not be a bad idea). The result of this overspecialization is that the individual tends to feel increasingly less in control vis-a-vis the totality of what is going on.

Less in control of what affects ones life in that she or he must depend on so many others for the great number of goods and services that go with living in a complex society. Only in societies of the simple life can the members provide for most of their own needs. If there ever was a society in which one could be a "Jack of all trades" it most certainly is not in ours. There is a kind of paradox in this since specialists, because they are such tend to think of themselves as important. And frequently they are, which should bolster their feeling of themselves as worthwhile. But along with the feeling of lack of control, overspecialization (constant repetition of the same narrowed tasks) tends toward boredom in one's specialty (is this at least partly responsible for one of our newest growing social problems - "burn-out"?). Feelings of lack of control and of boredom seem frequently to diminish if not overcome whatever feelings of worthwhileness one might get from feeling important as a specialist. In short, so many seem to get the feeling of being (or becoming) shrinking cogs in the rapidly growing gears of society.

(A brief digression from Simmel. In addition to adapting to rapid change and over-complexity there seems to be another factor promoting both the feeling of a lack of control and of boredom. That is the clear expectation that we succeed economically, as individuals. As such we are put on our own, standing alone. While this could allow us to have a great deal of control over what happens to us it is also frequently seen as threat and threats do not ordinarily enhance our feeling of being in control. It can also be seen as involved with feelings of boredom with work. Since the expectation is for economic success it tends to have many of us select occupations exclusively for their promise of great economic reward. Entering an occupation without a real interest in the work involved is frequently an entrance into boredom, "burn out." A very large number of American college students are enrolled in business programs; a large number are planning on careers as lawyers and physicians. While obviously these are very worthwhile goals, occupations that can be very rewarding in themselves, I often wonder about the real motive of many who are preparing for them.)

So far, Simmel's theory paints a rather dismal picture of modern society. But is boredom, the lack of feeling of control, or worse, the dehumanizing blase personality, all we can look forward to? Simmel doesn't seem to think so. The very process that seems to condemn us may be that which can correct our situation. Individuals could be forced, by these very negative experiences, deeper into themselves where they would discover their true selves, their own worthwhileness for who they are as persons regardless of what they do or what is going on in their overall societies.

But why would the true self be worthwhile? In another place (Wolff, p. 62) he distinguishes between two kinds of values: social and human. Social values are those we get from society, from "what is going on." Human values, he implies, are basic to human nature. Included in these are kindness and a sense of nobility of character.

These are what we would find when we get beyond hiding in to looking inside ourselves.

(This idea, that human beings are basically positively oriented, has been strongly supported by a number of more recent writers as a result of their many years experience as therapists dealing with problems of mental health: among them are Abraham Maslow, Carl Rogers, Rollo May, Erich Fromm and Arthur Janov.)

Looking inside, concentrating on ourselves, may, on the surface, appear to be a step toward individualism. But for Simmel, this could be a positive thing, could in itself lead not only to a better life for the individual but for everyone, for society. In short, it could get us beyond the negative selfishness we ordinarily associate with individualism.

The benefit to the individual in discovering these positive inner qualities is obvious. But why the benefit to all? Why would it go beyond negative selfishness? First, since the affects of over-stimulation and extreme specialization pervade the society itself they are felt by virtually all. Virtually all would then tend to be forced inside self where the feeling of worthwhileness would be discovered. But more than this. A further discovery would be made; that is, that this positive feeling deep inside us is the result of the positive experiences we've had with others. An awareness of this would tend us to see that what we do, of itself, is not what gives us the feeling of worthwhileness but that this feeling is directly connected to the quality of our relationship with others. Our idea of ourselves as persons is our idea of who we are in the eyes of other persons. (A notion closely related to Cooley's "Looking Glass Self.") That others are far more important to us than things, including the things we do. And, of course, it is axiomatic that the way to enjoy a good relationship with others is to be good to them. A widespread mutual exercise of being good to others quite obviously would benefit all. This is a benefit to all that comes not, as it did in many earlier settings, from all behaving in conformity with one another by living in conformity with a virtually complete set of societal norms. A benefit bought at the price of very little freedom of behavior. No, the benefit that Simmel writes of is based squarely on individualism. An individualism that benefits all because all are related to as who they are as persons. Where the only requirement for conformity is that all would respect all for who they are, would relate to one another first as persons and not as performers.

Here we can see a correspondence with Durkheim's notion of organic solidarity: that specialization (while not oppressive in itself as Simmel believed) would lead us to a feeling of union with others not as specialists (performers) but as sharing in a common humanity, as persons.

Here also there appears to be a close parallel with what Cooley saw as the origin of the feeling of worthwhileness. The experience of positiveness (the experience of who one is) in our primary relations with others produces a feeling of worthwhileness (the happy child, pleased with her or himself). For Simmel, introspection could return this feeling to us. And to the extent that it does it would overcome the effects of being conditioned to feel about ourselves mainly in terms of what we accomplish. A return, or at least a returning, to the stage of enjoying <u>oneself</u> through enjoying others, through being respected by and respecting others.

Was Simmel on to something (even if it took a

generation or two, after he wrote, to surface)? Some recent sociological evidence indicates that he was. Daniel Yankelovich published the results of research his organization conducted in 1973 involving a national sample of over 3,500 American young people between the ages of 16 and 25, roughly one-third of whom were college students. Among the variety of topics probed were the values that were personally very important to the respondents. Each was asked to list these values which were then ranked according to how often they appeared throughout the total sample (p. 90). Ranked 1, 2, and 3 were love, friendship, and fulfillment as a person; love appearing on the lists of 88 percent and 87 percent of the non-college and college people respectively, friendship 87 percent and 86 percent, and fulfillment as a person 87 percent for both groups. Work (fairly obviously a reference to <u>what one does</u>) appeared on only 53 percent of the non-college lists, 43 percent of the college. Given the almost identical scores for the top three rankings strongly suggest that for our young people in general self-fulfillment (<u>who one is</u> as a person) is strongly connected to, if not equated with, personal relationships.

It would seem that Simmel was certainly on to something when we add to the above data not only the claim of the therapists mentioned above (their common conclusion, after many years of practice, that human nature is basically oriented to friendliness) but also the result of recent experimental research conducted by several psychologists; research on the phenomenon of positive behavior. Among them is Professor Ervin Staub (University of Massachusetts) who finds that people treated in a friendly or kindly manner (for who they are) are prone not only to return friendliness and acts of kindness but to extend them to others; suggesting a natural attraction toward positiveness. Staub actually states that those who are helped are prone to help. I'm substituting friendliness and kindness since all three have one thing in common, of extending positiveness to another as a person. When we are helped don't we tend to see this as a gesture toward us as persons? That regardless of what the helping act is it is motivated by an intention to help <u>us</u>. That the helper recognizes that it is you or I as persons who need the help. And when we help others don't we intend it toward them <u>as persons</u>? Helping or being helped by strangers clearly illustrates this. Strangers have no personal knowledge of one another. By definition they do not know each other. But the one thing a helping stranger does know about the other is that he or she is a person, a person who needs help. Extending positiveness, through one's own person, to the person of the other. The attraction of person to person.

Simmel's basic thesis is also supported by the psychiatrist William Glasser who, writing in the early 1970s, claims that in general, the relatively economically secure people of the Western World are increasingly putting "acceptance as persons" ahead of recognition for task performance (p. 1,2).

Some might point to the great interest of today's students in occupation oriented college programs as indicating a reversal of what Glasser observed fifteen years ago or even what the Middletown study revealed ten years ago. I don't think so, for two reasons. The first, students today certainly are interested in getting good jobs but, as intimated earlier in this chapter, it seems that good jobs can be translated good money and good money seems to them to translate to access to having good times. The

18

second (certainly related to the first): while they don't neglect their college work, they spend a lot of time having a good time "hanging out" with their friends, simply being with one another. This is the source of their real self-fulfillment, their main value; and I don't see much (if any) more of a challenge to this value from future occupations than there is now from college work. This is not to be taken as a negative judgement on their value; in fact, I admire them, I envy them.

What is significant is that, in agreeing on fulfillment through positive relations with one another as the direction in which our social life is heading, Simmel, Durkheim and Cooley are assuming something in our nature that promotes this. This should not be surprising: Few would deny (especially not a sociologist) that our nature is social; that in order to develop into typically functioning human beings we have an absolute need for the generally positive atmosphere of a society. But a prerequisite for forming and maintaining any society is the predominance of the exchange of positiveness; a society characterized by an ongoing exchange of negativeness is inconceivable (this is why Northern Ireland is not one society, but two). The mutual feeling of belonging, of acceptance, a required characteristic in any adequate definition of society, comes only from the exchange of positiveness. What I am suggesting by all this is that to say that our nature is social means not only that we have a need for and are conditioned by society but that there is something in our nature (something we are born with) that seeks (orients us toward) the positive experience of society; something which society could not exist without since society is a collective product of that universally observable seeking.

To avoid any misunderstanding about what I have just

said it must be made clear that stating that a society characterized by negativeness is an impossibility does not mean that negativeness is not part of societal life but that no society can be based on it. And the claim that society depends on something we are born with means that the existence of society depends on that orientation or seeking we are born with, but one that can be actualized only in society.

CHAPTER 3
Pitirim A. Sorokin

Pitirim A. Sorokin lived through some interesting, if stormy, experiences during his earlier life in his native Russia. He was Professor of Sociology at the University of St. Petersburg. In 1917, he became secretary to Alexander Kerensky when Kerensky was the leader of the provisional government following the initial Russian revolution. Before this, Sorokin had been imprisoned several times by the Czarist regime and after the fall of the Kerensky government, he became a target of the regime of Lenin. His sentence to death by the latter was commuted to banishment and in 1923 he came to the United States. Here he taught at the University of Minnesota from 1924 to 1930 when he went to Harvard University. In 1931, he founded the Department of Sociology at Harvard where he was its head for roughly fifteen years and, after this, remained a professor of sociology until his retirement in 1955.

Sorokin (like Cooley, Durkheim, Simmel and Park) was concerned in a major way with the quality of morality in society.

Eleven years after going to Harvard, his The Crisis of Our Age was published; a monument to his convictions concerning sociology. It is from this work that I present my interpretation of Sorokin. Rather, this is not really an interpretation (he was far too straightforward to lend himself to, or need, interpretation by anyone) but an application of his theoretical ideas to our present society.

His social analysis in The Crisis of Our Age is based on a three part model (he actually had a fourth one but it is not important for our discussion); three different cultures

21

one of which tends to dominate in a society at any given time.

Very briefly these can be described as follows. The ideational culture is one in which the belief dominates that the answers to life's biggest questions ("What is happiness?; "How are we fulfilled?") come only from non-empirical (non-quantifiable, non-measurable) sources; from meaningful ideas that in themselves are satisfying, fulfilling. Typically, these ideas come from theology or philosophy. The sensate culture is the opposite of the ideational. There the dominating belief is that the answers to those questions come only from the material, quantifiable, measurable sources. Typically, these answers come from science and technology. The idealistic culture combines the other two; the belief that the answers can come and do come from either source.

He identified the early Middle Ages of Europe as an example of the ideational; most of the Western World of today as sensate. For a time, in the transition from then to now, the idealistic existed. While he certainly favored a return to the idealistic he recognized that during the periods of domination of both the ideational and sensate cultures much good had been realized in the form of worthwhile theological/philosophical ideas and scientific advances.

The problem with both these cultures is that neither addresses the totality of the reality of humanity. Our nature seeks meaning through ideas, especially religious ideas. Even Freud, while considering them illusions, recognizes that religious ideas - specifically of God and immortality (p. 58) - provide satisfaction for "the most urgent wishes" of humanity (p. 52). But these most urgent desires, or our seeking meaning, satisfaction in any such

22

ideas cannot be satisfied in a sensate culture since they have no place in it. On the other hand, our nature quite obviously has a desire for personal physical satisfaction, and to know about our physical world. Clearly the ideational culture offers no help here. This is why societies tend to move from one of these cultural forms toward the other; that is, when the desires of "half" our nature have been too long unsatisfied. In moving toward but not to either of these extremes the other possibility is open for stopping the movement in the middle - settling permanently into the idealistic culture.

A classic example of a missed opportunity to help bring about that possibility: the earlier idea of geocentrism, that the Earth was located at the center of the world, was for theologians an ideational one in that they reasoned that our central position in all of creation was a sign of God's special love for humanity. And for a time "science" seems to have had no quarrel with geocentrism. But along came Copernicus and, aided by the technology of the telescope, Galileo. Geocentrism was proven beyond doubt to be false. And this is where the missed opportunity comes in - a miss that set the Western World on its course well past the idealistic to the sensate culture.

Instead of realizing that they were facing irrefutable evidence and that geocentrism was not necessary at all as a sign of God's love for humanity the church leaders bristled at being told they were wrong. In their rage they condemned Galileo (as if this would change the scientific fact he had firmly established); Copernicus "escaped" by dying at the time his theory was published.

In short, in stubbornly, arrogantly refusing to recognize the validity of this proven scientific idea they missed the opportunity to cooperate with science, missing at least the chance to promote an ongoing idealistic culture.

As science increased its discoveries, its leaders too attained the equally arrogant attitude of absolute conviction that their position, their methodology, was the only one that reveals the true reality of anything. Be that as it may, the die was cast and by the 19th century science, because of the position of respect (awe?) it attained through its claims about the reality of nature and the obviously beneficial technology it produced, caused the pendulum to swing far from the ideational. (Interestingly, Max Plack, the father of quantum physics, firmly states (1959, p. 43) that all the wonderful advances in science reveal nothing of the true reality--the reality in itself--of anything.)

The sensate culture is very much the dominant one of our society and many others. Sorokin saw that we were so saturated with it that he referred to it as over-ripe. He also referred to it as being in its "dying days', indicating that he saw that we were ready for another shift. (However he also thought that we might not get a chance to do so because of the increasing destructiveness of wars. And when he wrote The Crisis of Our Age in 1941 he knew nothing of the potential for the absolute destructiveness of the "pride" of the sensate, nuclear weaponry.)

But while the sensate may be in its dying days an announcement of its death would certainly be premature. We need only look around us, within us, to see how much life it still has. Materialism is very much part of our lives. Ours is called a consumer society for very good reason. Many of us are in occupations that involve working with ideas that could in themselves be a source of satisfaction, but so many see their job satisfaction not in these ideas but almost entirely in the money they realize from their work. Translated: satisfaction from how well they consume; how many material things and physical pleasures they can afford. Success in our society is clearly equated with this.

For some examples let's begin with my own occupation. What happened to the professor who developed and wrote about her or his ideas without a grant (without extra income) to support what should be an intellectually motivated endeavor? I have difficulty imagining Durkheim saying to himself that he would love to write a book on the sociology of religion but that he wouldn't even start his research without a grant from some foundation. Or that he would never consider writing more than the first chapter without an advance from a publisher. And Durkheim was not unique in his day. It seems safe to assume that he and others found their ideas rewarding in themselves, satisfying in themselves. I am certainly not coming out against grants or advances, or the people seeking them. The problem is that they have become so much part of our academic experience that it seems to be taken for granted (pun intended) that ideas cannot (or at least should not) be developed without them. The attitude of an increasing number in the academic profession (among many others) seems to be that material rewards are a definite prerequisite to the further development of ideas.

In addition to the above there is another way in which the sensate, materialistic culture has invaded academic circles; specifically those that are technologically and business oriented. In the former the ideas that are developed involve making or building things; making more

25

progress in the material world is the real reason for their development. Obviously such progress is good (although nuclear weaponry certainly wouldn't qualify here) but again the problem is the strong tendency to value ideas only in so far as they serve a materialistic goal. And with business education, materialism is at the heart of the matter; virtually all its ideas are satisfying only in so far as they promote profit and income.

This same phenomenon can be seen in many other occupations. Material gain as the main barometer of fulfillment seems to be a growing attitude in the medical and legal professions. There seems to be little fulfillment in the idea of being a good physician or attorney, unless it also involves the idea of a very good income. As indicated earlier, in more than just a few cases there can be great suspicion about which of these goods is the major attraction for the aspirants to these and other high paying professions. The point is certainly not that the idea of satisfaction from a very good income is a dishonorable one (it clearly isn't) but that its emphasis tends to stand in the way of choosing a profession because of interest in the ideas inherent in it.

Another dimension of this is the quite general lack of interest that students have in pursuing ideas as such, ideas not directly related to their professional preparation. And why should they considering the interest our materialistic culture promotes. Not only our culture in general but at least some areas of it directly connected to education. A friend of mine recently submitted his manuscript in sociology for publication. He was informed by the publisher that the three sociologists who reviewed his work objected that it was too theoretical and conceptual. In short, it contained too many ideas; although only one of seven chapters was devoted to theory. Sociologists at least used to know that the heart of sociology is theory. This observation can serve as a bridge to our next discussion about the sensualist dimension of the sensate culture. Our young people did not decide to reject the notion of satisfaction from ideas in themselves, they are simply seeking fulfillment. And, as we have already seen, the sensate culture, the very advanced stage of which has been the only experience of our youth, doesn't promote fulfillment through ideas. Since the sensate is their only experience they are the most saturated by it, and so best reflect the sensate fulfillment. Many of our older people find fulfillment and satisfaction in material things: fine food, fine cars, fine houses. While certainly not rejecting these things, young people best reflect fulfillment and satisfaction from a very closely related (but distinguishable) source of direct sensualism: direct stimulation of the senses themselves. This is clear in the affinity of so many of them for rock music; that is, in their attraction to the beat itself and most especially in the loudness of the beat. (This, like the other examples that follow, is not meant as a negative judgement. These examples are simply presented as illustrations of the sensate in our culture.) The point is that this music does not provide satisfaction so much through the melody or the words (ideas) themselves but basically through the decibels bombarding not only the sense of hearing, through the ears, but the sense of feeling, through the whole body. It is worth noting here that while the young embrace this experience as their own, it began with a number of earlier sensation seekers, classical music buffs. I can recall that over 30 years ago I visited a friend who had just purchased a stereo set. He insisted on seating me in a chair located

27

directly between the two speakers and proceeded to turn the thing all the way up for me to listen to the classical record he was playing (lots of kettle drums and cymbals, of course). When it was over (and my nerves were almost completely jangled) I asked why it had to be so loud; he responded that it was the only way to really appreciate it.

Owning and driving fast automobiles with powerful engines is certainly popular with many of our young. The satisfaction derived from these is clearly the thrill of the sense experience of speed itself and the noise and vibrations of a roaring engine. If it's objected that what they are really doing is simply "showing off" this doesn't change what I just said since what they'd be doing is trying to attract the attention of others who share their admiration for that sense satisfaction.

Violence for the sake of violence, having little if anything to do with a plot is quite common in our movies and television shows. Sex for the sake of sex, not to dramatize an idea central to the story (as it was for example in the movie, Born on the Fourth of July), is common (and blatantly obvious) in our movies, best selling novels and television shows (e.g., the afternoon "soaps"). Again, I am making no judgments about these portrayals in themselves, merely pointing them out as illustrations of our sensate culture. I do, however, have a strong negative judgment about the manipulation that lies behind them (e.g., making mere sex objects of women, or even men for that matter); and that they involve manipulation is made so obvious by the covers of most paperback novels and the ads for many of the films and television shows.

As stated earlier, Sorokin in viewing the sensate culture as being in its dying days looked for a shift. And there are signs that we may be turning toward an idealistic

28

culture. An idealistic culture since it is absolutely obvious that we could never return to the ideational because too much valuable knowledge and hardware have been and continue to be provided by our scientists and technologists. We could never again think of these as providing no fulfillment and satisfaction in our lives. Interestingly, science itself seems to be leading us toward the idealistic; much of the thinking in modern science, in quantum theory, is no longer as representative of the sensate as that which preceded it.

Among the useful hardware (itself sensate) is that which opened and continues to open the way for this revolutionary thinking (ideas) in modern science (e.g., the cyclotron; the radio telescope; the television microscope). Hardware that has given evidence for and pushed further the theories of some of the seminal thinkers of the modern science; those no longer restrained by the basically mechanistic views that dominated earlier science. Those who differ from their predecessors in that they, while not relinquishing their task of endlessly pursuing knowledge, are convinced that whatever that knowledge may be it will never be complete and that in itself it will involve dimensions of the mysterious (Barnett, p. 117). In fact, it is quite interesting that so many leading scientists seem to have been forced by their advance in scientific knowledge to turn "partial" philosopher, if not "partial" theologian. Einstein is a classic example: he maintains that no only is the sense of the mystical the heart of religiousness but its also the base of "all true science" (Barnett, p. 108). Max Planck, the father of quantum physics, wrote that while science must keep providing answers it had reached a stage where the ultimate "answers" can be approached only by "poetic intuition" (p. 83). And J. Robert Oppenheimer states that what we can observe and what we cannot ("timelessness", "eternity") complement one another, neither alone tell us of reality.

I am particularly fond of the above since they so well embody the characteristics of the idealistic culture: the value of science and the value of ideas that lie beyond what science can explain. The partly sensory; partly super-sensory or ideational.

Consider the mystery (the complete incompre-hensibleness) of a current description of the center of a black hole; that is, that which has infinite mass and zero volume. Wow! Is this not a good match in terms of mystery for one God who is described as a trinity? Are not the scientists the new providers of mystery? An interesting way of looking at this is that quantum theory is undoing some basic assumptions of classic science, just as the latter earlier had done to religion.

What we have been dealing with so far involves the avant-garde of science. The vast majority of us (including many teachers of science) have not grasped the real significance of the ideas of these leaders of science. To this extent we tend to continue to view all science as firmly based in only the sensate. But there is other evidence of our looking for meaning in the ideational as well as the sensate that involves a good number of us.

Very rapidly growing in popularity are motion pictures very different from those characteristic of the sensate. Those that feature the "unearthly," the mysterious: E.T., Star Wars, The Empire Strikes Back, The Return of the Jedi, Close Encounters Of the Third Kind, Poltergeist, The Amityville Horror, The Exorcist, etc. What is significant about these movies is not that they were produced but that they attracted such a very large following; in many cases people have seen some of them two, three, and more times. And it does not seem tenable to assume that most patrons of these films are attracted to nothing more that the "special effects" they contain.

Books of a similar vein that were not made into movies have also attracted a very large readership. Books of the genre of Heinlein's <u>Stranger in a Strange Land</u>; those that deal with good, positive, helpful "people" who came from other places, from mysterious places. A further significance of these movies and books is that whatever is mystery presented remains a mystery at the end. In contrast consider how most frequently the mystery or unearthliness in earlier popular books or movies was usually completely solved or at least the figure representing them was destroyed, e.g., Dracula, Frankenstein, The Thing. Also, the unearthly figures of the past were almost invariably all evil. These differences seem significant as evidence of a movement toward the idealistic, precisely because they indicate that many people today seem to be fascinated by (attracted to) mystery that remains mystery that is beyond human power to solve; that while comfortable with their material life, they seem attracted to the unearthly.

Another phenomenon that is of interest in this regard is the popularity, especially among our young women, of paperback romance novels; an indication that satisfaction is being derived from them. This is significant since nothing in our experience lends itself less to measurement or rational definition that romantic love (the Masters and Johnson electrodes don't have a reading for this). There simply is no rational scientific way of conveying the meaning of love. However, since romantic stories were written and read (and later viewed on the screen) throughout the height of our sensate culture their current popularity may not indicate a movement from the sensate as such but rather that romance, for a good reason, has always stood in opposition to both extreme cultures. Romantic love is a classic example of idealistic satisfaction since while it is clearly a spiritual phenomenon it is also clearly built on the physical. All this would seem to indicate that we are attracted to the promise of something more than purely physical existence. Something that brings our physical existence into wholeness. Durkheim offers a thoughtful reflection related to this. While making it clear that facts gotten from science are important, he states that this is insufficient. Scientific knowledge evolves too slowly, remains too incomplete to provide a holistic explanation of life. Such explanations can come only from religion (1965, p. 479). Like Einstein, Planck and Oppenheinmer, he too sees the value of explanations from both the sensate and the ideational.

What we have discussed in this chapter suggests to me at least the beginnings of our movement toward the idealistic culture.

CHAPTER 4
Robert Ezra Park

Robert Ezra Park graduated from the University of Michigan in 1887. It is quite likely that some of his ideas on the reform of society were due to the influence of the philosopher John Dewey who was teaching there at the time. (Cooley graduated from that university in the same year and although his undergraduate work was in engineering it is quite possible that he too was affected by Dewey's philosophy of society.)

Park (in his article "Human Ecology") writes of the comparison between human behavior and that of other forms of animal life. In a manner similar to several writers today, he indicates that human behavior involves a sublimination or higher refinement of some of the traits of other animals. However, unlike many of the current writers, he is very clear in seeing our behavior as qualitatively different in that he understands the motivation if not always the observable patterns of human behavior to be very distinguishable from that of other forms of animal life.

The areas of some similarity between the human and these other forms of life are located on what Park refers to as the biotic level. This is the level characterized by a kind of blind striving for survival; a classic example being competition for living space. "Reflections" of this obvious trait of so many forms of life (territoriality) can be seen in the competition for living space among human populations. As an example, he refers to the typical pattern of spatial movement of many American ethnic groups. That is, settling initially, as immigrants, in the least desirable residential areas near the center of a city; then later, by

33

displacing groups which frequently earlier had displaced other groups, they move progressively toward the edges of the city and ultimately to its suburbs. (This is an interesting example since by the time they reach the suburbs "they" are no longer immigrants but descendants of immigrants and typically they are not competing as ethnic groups. The so-called hyphenated Americans in the vast majority of today's suburbs do not live in groups, they are interspersed with the descendants of many different immigrant groups. Suburbia has become, to a large extent, the setting of the residential "melting pot." One glaring deficiency remains in all this, however, and that is our general reluctance to allow access to this setting to all our races.)

In any event, it is important to understand that Park's discussion of competition between groups of humans is for him only a reflection of blind competition since he states that humans never live at the biotic level as such but that our competition is carried out on what he calls the cultural level. That is, that human behavior is not something determined by our nature to be blindly acted out but that a properly functioning culture conditions it toward the restriction of competition, toward cooperation based on consensus; promotes our natural orientation toward positiveness, cooperation, by conditioning to forms of competition acceptable to all and conducted in fairness to all.

Analyzing how well the culture of any society promotes our nature is facilitated by Park in that he divided the cultural level into three ascending levels or orders: the economic, the political and the moral; where each is to function as a control over the level below it. What follows is my interpretation and application of his model. In a healthy society the economic level prevents activity that is based on the force of sheer economic manipulation that would be a mimacry of activity on the biotic level. The political level (political leadership) is to be the watchdog of the economic, assuring that it functions as it should. The moral level (the strength of which is determined by the degree of consensus of the society's members) is the authority for the political; exerting pressure on it to conduct the society in fairness to all its members. That is, the exercise of authority on the political level should prevent any competition on the economic level that is harmful to any segment of the society's membership or to the society as a whole, either of which would divide the members.

In this we can see that in practice the key is the political order since if it fails to function properly thereby dividing the membership, it weakens the legitimate source of its authority, the moral level.

In short, Park can be seen as suggesting that any society, if it is in the long run to remain a true representative of all its members, must allow for competition only as limited within the framework of consensus. That is, it must be characterized by a consensus on fairness since a society by definition is an entity within which there is at least to some degree a general feeling of belonging; a feeling possible only where there is a general agreement on basic fairness. (This is related to what was noted earlier: territories within which an exchange of positiveness does not predominate really contain several societies - e.g., again, the two societies of the "society" of Northern Ireland).

What can we say about our society in terms of these three levels?

First let us look at the devastating results of instances where manipulative economic competition was allowed to go on at least somewhat as the result of the improper operation of the economic and political orders.

The draft riot of 1863 is a good example. For almost five days in the middle of July 1863, the City of New York was completely taken over by bands of rioting Irish. The police force (also largely Irish) was almost immediately put to flight. Even locally based federal troops were ineffective in their attempt to subdue the rioters. Eventually, but only after Lincoln ordered more troops into the city, it was regained. As with many riots, there was much looting (one favorite target seems to have been Brooks Brothers clothing store); setting of fires (including several draft boards, Horace Greeley's New York Tribune office, and an occupied orphanage for Black children); and, general destruction of life and property. (It is interesting to note that an event of such magnitude -- mob rule of the country's largest city for the better part of a week during the war to preserve the nation -- seems to have gotten lost in our history books. I first heard of it only about twenty years ago. That is quite remarkable since I had several levels of courses in U.S. history during my long stretch of formal schooling that began in 1931. Even more remarkable is that it seems that after its brief surfacing - during draft card burning days of the late 1960s and early 1970s - it has submerged again. Over the past six years when discussing the incident with them, I have asked my Sociology of Community students if they ever heard of it. Only twelve of the approximately 850 of them said they had.)

Keeping in mind Park's insistence that a well ordered society could be achieved only if each of the social orders were reasonably controlled by the one above it. How, then, can his model aid in analyzing what really was a leading cause of the draft riot?

On the surface it appears, like most all riots appear, to be simply the result of the spread of discontent throughout an unruly, ungovernable mob. But why the discontent? Well, it could have been due to resistance to the first military draft we ever had. This would appear to be an unreasonable reaction since the decision in the political order was made to assure the military strength of the Union army. This certainly was the aim of the political order but in its efforts it failed not only to control the economic order, but itself made improper use of that order. To spell it out, this is what was going on. The rioters, mostly day laborers or unemployed, felt economically deprived in an economic order that showed little or no concern for those at the bottom; an order where economic might was the rule. The political order did nothing to correct this source of discontent; it failed here to exercise reasonable control of the economic order. In addition, and adding fuel to the fire, the political order in enacting the draft legislation included an economic dimension that reinforced the inequities already existing in the economic order. Anyone who was drafted and could put up $300 did not have to go into the military. For the most part the Irish could not afford the $300. Not only was their lowly economic status already a source of discontent, now it could mean being killed in the war. What do you think that might do to one's level of discontent? (The end of the story: the political order got the city back and the draft was peacefully resumed shortly after this - but without the condition of "buying out" for $300. An interesting lesson for those today who decry the

37

government's "giving in" to the demands of minorities.) There was another brutal element to this incident. Aside from the destruction of life and property, there were racial overtones. In addition to the incident of the orphanage, many Blacks and abolitionists were singled out for brutal treatment by the rioters; an action for which the mob cannot be excused. But even here the lack of reasonable control by the political over the economic played a large part in promoting the extremes of racial hatred. The government had not only tolerated but legalized slavery, the buying and selling of people, in the economic order. The federal government itself was openly engaged in racism; racism that was applied to our Native Americans as well, where it had genocide in mind. Control by the political order, especially in one that calls itself a democratic republic, is supposed to be exercised over the economic order in the interest of all over whom the government has power. Today we seem to have a somewhat better notion of this. We have federal laws that are designed to prevent racial discrimination and, to some degree, economic manipulation of any of our people. At least we do not legally allow people to be mistreated in these areas. This is a very important step because while you "cannot legislate love" (and nobody ever said you could) we can and did legislate hate. At least that obstacle to enhancing our moral order has been removed.

There were many other riots in our history (many of them labor riots in the latter part of the 19th century, involving a variety of poor white ethnics) and if we analyze them in terms of these orders, we find the same deficiency in the political control or misuse of the economic level. (If anyone is wondering why I capitalize the word Black but not white it is because that term, in the U.S., designates an ethnic group, white does not. White ethnic groups are also capitalized; Italian -- or Irish-American, etc.) Our more recent urban riots are clearly the result of this deficiency since they are clearly the results of economic inequities allowed to exist far too long by lack of political control over our economic level. The political level did attempt correction of some of the problem when it enacted the National Labor Relations Act, and it was quite effective in our society in general. But there was a cruel irony in this, too. Labor unions, the legalized vehicles that were to provide economic help for so many, were allowed to practice their own brand of manipulation in the economic order. With very few exceptions they were allowed, by one means or another, to exclude from their ranks racial minorities; and they did. And this practice of exclusion prevailed from 1935 to quite recently (while significantly limited, it is still not completely gone); extending, unhampered by our federal political order, well past the time (beginning after World War II) when so many others were significantly improving their economic lot. Improving it by a legally allowed "de facto" quota system for decent incomes - 100% white (another lesson for those today who think quota systems unfair).

It is even more complicated. This is the same period in which technologically and economically we shifted away from an emphasis on manual labor; the labor that had kept the bulk of the white population economically viable from at least the end of the Civil War to the end of World War II. Jobs now require much higher levels of formal education. But even to this day the minorities, in far greater numbers than whites, do not get a decent education. What is a major reason for this? Again, the answer lies in a deficiency on the part of the political order. Most frequently the initial education experience (vital for any subsequent education) for minority children takes place in a neighborhood school; that seems reasonable and fair since it's what happens to virtually all children. The problem resides in the neighborhood schools themselves; in the great difference in the quality of education from one neighborhood to another. This difference in quality is itself largely economic in that, at least until quite recently, much less money was spent on the schools in minority neighborhoods. And why are there minority neighborhoods? Again, manipulation in the economic order is involved. We just saw how, as a group, racial minorities were kept out of the mainstream of our economic life. So generally, as a group, their incomes prevent them from living anywhere else; they are economically manipulated in a fashion similar to the Irish in New York City in 1863. In addition, when later some minorities did increase their incomes realtors and white residents were allowed to openly, if not legally, "keep them out." All the rhetoric about the lack of the spirit of delayed gratification or parental control (both of which the earlier Irish, too, were accused) as reasons for poor school performance pales significantly in the face of the much belated and still largely ineffective political control over our economic level concerning open housing.

One of the most common arguments heard is: "Our people worked hard to get where we are, why don't they?" Many of the immigrant groups and their children did work hard (although low-paying, after the Civil War there were usually plenty of unskilled jobs for them) but that's really not how they as groups got where they did. For the most part their economic advances were helped along by working, scrimping, but also fighting for what they got.

40

Most of us are familiar with the long list of labor riots and general labor unrest in the latter part of the last century and into the present one. What we frequently don't recognize is that these events usually involved groups of white immigrants or their sons. People who felt (and were) mistreated and <u>reacted violently</u> to this treatment.

In our own day the lack of reasonable control of the economic level continues to weaken our moral order. The activities of many of our oil companies and large conglomerates in general are excellent examples of free-wheeling economic manipulation and profiteering. The political policy of "trickle down" or "supply side" economics is based on <u>consciously</u> withholding control over the economic order. Another example was a recent President's insistence on blaming our inflationary condition on too much government spending which was ironic since his requests for the military were such a large part of our budget. While government spending was partly responsible it is not the reason inflation became such a problem. All we have to do is think back to the early seventies when our inflation zoomed skyward. It was the time of the oil "crunch" and government spending had nothing to do with precipitating this. And who were the recipients of the greatest profit from all this? The oil companies, of course. And, once inflation took its "big leap," others demanded more to meet their rising expenses; the spiral was on. It has damaged the lives of so many of our people, especially the poor in general and those on fixed incomes such as many of the retired elderly. And the boast that inflation has been significantly slowed is an additional insult to our people on low incomes since it has not slowed in areas most vital to them: housing, food, and health care.

Big unions, too, are part of this picture. The

41

unionized oil workers seemed quite willing to cooperate in inflated prices as long as they got their share; the auto workers, too, seemed to see little problem with soaring costs until an increasing number of people could no longer afford or simply refused to pay the prices asked for new automobiles, (or started buying foreign ones), and plants started closing.

It would seem that a reasonable (good for all) step for our political order to take to quiet our inflation problem would be a freeze, or better yet, a roll-back and freeze, "across the board" on profits, prices, rents, and wages; a war-time measure for a war on inflation. President Nixon's freeze on wages failed miserably. It was bound to. After all wages are not the only factor in inflation. And did he really expect the corporations to voluntarily freeze their prices and profits? Profit based on "whatever the traffic will bear" (the maximization of profits) has been a standard business practice for longer than anyone can remember. "The business of America is business."

Such an "across the board" roll-back and freeze (only temporary, but for at least two years; time for government and private yearly budgets to be adjusted at least twice) would stem inflation and do so without the loss of jobs. As extreme as this would be, it seems the only way to keep an increasing number of our people from being left out while others are enjoying the good life. And only when virtually all of our people feel that something is being done for them will our moral level be strengthened.

We are going to go deeper into trouble until we really become aware of the dangerous game we are playing and come to realize that no society can run well or even continue in existence without a relatively strong moral level. And our moral level is probably in more trouble than ever before since our communications system (especially television) informs virtually all our people of what is happening. An increasing number of our middle income people are beginning to feel more and more left out; joining the ranks of our poor who for even a better reason feel this way. Simmel observed that an increasingly complex culture leaves an increasing number of its participants behind in some aspects of knowledge but virtually all of us are becoming aware, through television, etc., of the economic inequities of our society. More and more people are perceiving themselves at least to some degree as victims of injustice; fewer and fewer are contented with the system. It is all up to the political level. Let that order consider seriously that it is responsible to all the members of society and that it alone can control the economic level. That as such it alone can pave the way for a healthy moral level. In all of this I am not suggesting that our political order (or any political order) will ever operate perfectly in this regard but a much better showing of good will, a much greater honest effort, would go a long way toward eliminating discontent.

CHAPTER 5
The Social Theorists and Religion

In this chapter we will apply the ideas of the social theorists we've been discussing to the phenomenon of religion. Religion is selected since as a major social institution it has been of specific interest to a number of sociologists and to sociology in general. As a social institution it interacts with society in general; therefore, what our theorists had to say about society should be at least somewhat applicable to religion.

In addition, in looking at them as they are related to the same phenomenon, we can further another aim of this book: to see to what extent the ideas of the theorists are related.

Cooley

Cooley saw that the experience of positiveness in the initial primary group typically only fairly satisfies our primary need; but that this is sufficient for orienting us toward our development as persons properly functioning in accordance with our nature. As only fairly satisfied, he can be seen as assuming that, since that need is basic to our nature, it is ongoing, always seeking further satisfaction. This could explain his primary ideals--thoughts of care and concern that indicate at least to some degree feelings of union not only with those with whom we come into contact but potentially with all human beings. Interestingly, the practice of the primary ideals is also an ideal of at least all the world's major religions; and an ongoing need for union would be finally satisfied only by the ultimate objective of these religions: union with union itself (God, Nirvana, etc.).

44

It is important to recall that since our nature orients but does not determine our behavior we can be taught not to be open to the extension of primary ideas. It is precisely in this that a contradiction can be seen in many religions. While care and concern for others in general is clearly stated in their scriptures as the ideal toward which all their members should strive, they tend to teach that the most important concern is the observance of a variety of detailed practices and disciplinary rules. Practices and rules that not only have nothing to do with the ideal but, as most important, tend to completely replace it or at least seriously detract from it.

Religions are looked upon by their adherents as guardians of ultimate human destiny; they are believed in and relied on as bearers of the ultimate plan for "salvation." Therefore, observance of the practices and rules tends to be accepted as completely sufficient for living a good life. A life that will merit whatever their particular religion calls "salvation". But the basic human condition, the human nature, that Cooley writes of (primary needs) should (when met by an at least satisfactory primary group experience) result in the extension of primary ideals. When these ideals are not reached by those whom religion has reduced to rules observers, then religion has not only thwarted human nature but, ironically, has discouraged these people from any progress at all toward its own ideal.

An example of this was very severely experienced within Roman Catholicism especially prior to the second Vatican Council (a major purpose of which was to correct this problem). It was quite common for many of its members to think of themselves as "good Catholics" since they faithfully observed the requirements for membership in "good standing." That is, if they went to Mass every Sunday and Holydays; to "the sacraments" at least once a year; observed all the details of fast and/or abstinence appropriate to the days designated as those requiring such penitential observance; and, contributed to the support of the parish. Charity was not <u>really thought of</u> (even by most of the clergy) as basically involving on-going care and concern (love) for all others; the "obligation" of charity was generally seen as limited to contributing occasionally to special collections for charitable purposes. But even this was more or less optional, not really an obligation. One was not made to fear God's displeasure for skipping on these collections (but such was not the case for those failing to contribute to the support of their parish). No, as long as they adhered to the above rules they were on the right track and needn't bother to extend care and concern for anyone but their own circle of family and possibly friends. Much of this picture has changed since the Council; there is <u>much more</u> official talk of more fully extending care and concern to any others in need. But it is still not made clear (as it certainly is in Matthew, 25) that failing to do so is an extremely serious neglect of an extremely serious command.

The same was probably true, changing only some of the details, in many other Christian religions (in the more fundamentalist of these - refraining from playing cards, going to the movies, swearing, drinking, etc. constituted the "good Christian life").

Cooley then is making an interesting, direct connection between the basic human condition and what are the stated official ideals of all major religions. In short, Cooley's claim that our nature itself is oriented toward positiveness (a claim supported by more recent

46

experimental research in psychology on altruism - a good survey of this is in D. Bar-Tal, <u>Prosocial Behavior</u>) is the official ideal of many religions. However it seems that the leaders of those religions for whatever reasons lost sight of what was supposed to be their ideal; a strange development for Christianity since that ideal is <u>so clearly</u> stated in Christian scripture.

It's interesting that a sociologist should have recognized this positive condition in human nature long before those Christian religions began to re-emphasize their ideal. Interesting but perhaps not so strange since sociologists in general fail to recognize the implications in Cooley's work. A failure that is difficult to understand since sociologists in general recognize human nature as social. A concept that in itself implies that our nature orients us toward positive relations with one another.

In the case of Catholicism, an awareness of and serious attention given to Cooley's work might have provided the motivation to re-emphasize the ideal more than fifty years before Vatican Two (then again if the basic command of scripture was ignored why would Cooley's ideas be valued?). But, then, if mainstream sociology itself never saw Cooley's model as relatable to religion (since it concerned itself only with his primary group) why would anyone else be expected to see the connection? Maybe the major reason why Cooley is never mentioned in books on the sociology of religion is not because he didn't concentrate on religion as such but because sociologists in general have ignored his two chapters on primary ideals, ignored his connection between human nature as social and the ideals of religion.

Durkheim

For Durkheim religion is the symbolic representation of the feeling of solidarity shared by the people of a society. As such it is meaningful to them, it is their religion.

However, he also recognized that the horizons of the feeling of solidarity were increasingly widening beyond societal lines toward a trans-societal wholity; a process which we'll also refer to as social convergence. (Social convergence represents a change in terminology from societal convergence which I used in my earlier interpretation of Durkheim in Friendliness and Social Nature. I've decided that societal convergence can be misleading since the convergence does not involve societies as such but a convergence in friendliness and friendship of individuals across societal lines resulting in their feeling of social solidarity. It is a convergence toward a new social phenomenon, a trans-societal wholity.) How accurate is Durkheim's claim concerning religion as the symbolic representation of the experience of social solidarity? First we'll look at some examples in which a shared feeling of solidarity resulted in a particular religion as its representation. Following that we'll discuss a variety of examples that are related to his basic idea of the affect of social convergence on religion.

(Some of these examples refer to national societies and others to societies within nations so it must be made clear that for Durkheim a society is any horizon within which the feeling of solidarity is restricted. Therefore, ethnic groups in an ethnically pluralistic nation that felt a solidarity only with "their own" would be separate societies within that nation.)

48

The spread of the single religion of Christianity throughout the Roman Empire doesn't seem (any more than the army of that empire) to have generated any real feeling of solidarity between the various groups or "nations" involved. There doesn't seem to have been any significant social convergence of these groups as evidenced by what happened at the breakup of Christianity. The various denominations that resulted from the Reformation most frequently became the representatives of the feeling of solidarity already existing within each of the various particular societies. (And, to the extent that social convergence has not yet taken place, they continue to function as such.) The society of England represented by Anglicanism; Scotland by Presbyterianism; Wales by Calvinistic Methodism; the Societies of Northern Germany, Denmark, Norway and Sweden by Lutheranism. This latter case is interesting in that it too indicates the power of societal (secular) life to affect religion. Even the sharing of the "same" religion did not mean that there was a feeling of solidarity between these societies. They continued to be influenced only by their own separate social solidarities in that the Lutheran church in each of these countries is completely autonomous. Interestingly, the Lutheran World Federation (while not a governing body it does involve cooperation) was not formed until after World War II; possibly because of the beginnings at that time of an exchange of positiveness between a significant number of the people of these former enemy or at least antagonistic societies (probably triggered by the experience of the Nazi regime). But even when mutually hostile societies shared the centrally governed Roman Catholicism (e.g., France and England before the Reformation) Durkheim's notion is not contradicted since

49

in those days the secular leaders selected the official religious leaders (bishops) of their respective societies; in short, these societies enjoyed a good measure of practical as well as official religious autonomy.

That Ireland remained strongly Roman Catholic after the Reformation (and is so to this day) is probably not completely unrelated to its absolute lack of a feeling solidarity with England. In any case, it is fairly evident that the feelings of solidarity are feelings directed toward respective societies; and that where these feelings are strong religion seems quite powerless to unite them.

What follows involves the effect on religion when the inter-societal contacts became sufficiently numerous, when the horizons of social solidarity were significantly extended toward a wholity. Prior to the end of World War II the great proportion of ethnic groups in the United States (hyphenated Americans and those considering themselves to be the "real Americans") lived in city or town neighborhoods made up only or largely of "their own." Separated from one another spatially and a great extent socially. Park described Chicago of the 1920s - as "a mosaic of little worlds"; worlds apart, worlds unto themselves, in a real sense, little <u>societies</u>. For many of our older cities and towns this is still somewhat the case. And to the extent to which these conditions exist the various religions tend to be quite antagonistic toward one another.

Shortly after World War II several changes began to occur. The rise of multi-ethnic neighborhoods in suburbia, increasing multi-ethnic populations in our colleges (the G.I. bill) and work places. As a result of these changes so many more of us today (especially our young people whose whole life experience has been in suburbia and who we

50

send to college in increasingly greater numbers) than formerly seem quite unconcerned about the national origin or religion of our friends. Does it seem purely accidental that it was only after this spatial and social convergence that the various religions of our country began their ecumenical discussions and activities? Isn't it very likely that this phenomenon is a response to strong ethnic barriers being lowered if not totally dismantled? People no longer seem comfortable with their religions so separated, let alone antagonistic toward each other, when they no longer feel any real separateness between themselves.

Interestingly this same process can be seen with those of the same official religion. For example the Italian, Polish, Irish, Slovak ethnic groups in general profess allegiance to Roman Catholicism. But they too seem to give evidence for Durkheim's thesis. To see this we have to understand that according to Durkheim's thinking sharing the same religious name or title but not a feeling of solidarity would mean not really sharing the same religion; we already saw this regarding Lutheranism in Germany, Sweden, etc. The present case is particularly interesting in that Roman Catholicism has always been claimed to be one under one authority, Rome. But did the Catholic ethnics in the United States really share the same religion? Do some of the older ones even today? While Rome firmly turned down a movement in the 1880s to rearrange the dioceses of the United States along ethnic lines it allowed, even promoted ethnically oriented parishes. Many officially designated as national parishes. Parishes where people had a strong feeling of belonging, but only with "their own." They did not welcome Catholics of other nationality backgrounds and were not welcomed by them. Somebody else's Catholic church was not their Catholic church. While greatly diminished generally after World War II some of this still persists mainly now especially among older people in ethnic neighborhoods that remain intact. For instance, twenty years after the war, in the city of Gary, Indiana, twenty-five of the forty-five parishes were ethnically oriented. And a student of mine who graduated only a few years ago, in discussing his upstate Pennsylvania small city (with five ethnic Catholic parishes) noted that mainly the older people still saw their parish as the only one for them while for the young all the churches were simply Catholic churches. Again the difference in the generations involved social convergence. It is the young who are mixing so much more with "others," increasingly forming friendships across the "lines" of ethnic societies, especially in regional high schools and colleges. The point is that all ages felt a strict allegiance only to their parishes while all their members were socially isolated from those of other ethnic groups, of other parishes; such allegiance was no longer characteristic of the young only after they experienced social convergence.

Research of my own also indicates that friendships (exchanges of the feeling of union) to a large extent are being formed across lines of ethnicity. That not only are potential friends very increasingly no longer being judged by nationality but that they represent a number of religions. In an in-class project I tell my students that they are to be married in six months. In preparation for this event I ask them to make a wedding reception list of those friends who are so close to them, such good friends, that they definitely want these people with them on this very special occasion. And I make it clear that only those who are their good friends are to be listed, that they're not to include any friends of friends through obligation. Only after they have completed their lists do I have them indicate (among other things) the nationality background and religion of each friend they've invited. Next they total the number of nationalities and religions. Over the past three semesters (total: 141 students) the results have been: 95% had friends of 2 or more nationality backgrounds other than their own, 48% had 4 or more. Forty percent indicated one religion other than their own; 45% indicated 2 or 3 other than theirs.

(This section is enclosed is parentheses since, although it is pertinent to the movement toward wholity, it is not related to change in religion. While it should be self-evident to most of us today, the following is research evidence of the increase in friendship across the lines of ethnic societies. It is hardly arguable that typically, at least in the United States, some level of friendship is a prerequisite for marriage, or that what the younger people are doing differently indicates the direction of change. Richard Alba, after analyzing data published by the National Opinion Research Center, states (p. 424) that in 1963 82% of Irish, 65% of Polish, and 69% of Italian Catholics, under age 31, had married across ethnic lines. While for those over 50 at that time, 74, 46, and 27 percent had married those of a different ethnicity. These data demonstrate a significant increase in roughly 20 years in inter-ethnic friendship. An increase in union across ethnic societal lines; an increase in the movement toward wholity. Although restricted to a wholity within our country, it is significant in that it illustrates what happened to diverse groups of people when brought into social contact with one another.)

In general, increasing social convergence, increasing awareness of unity of the people of the various social

53

groupings does seem to be leading to increasing unity of religions at least in the minds of the lay members. A unity in which religions retain their own identity, not converging into uniformity (this of course does not pertain to the young Catholic "ethnics" who now with few exceptions see themselves as de facto members of the same religion). This increase in social convergence that increasingly affects the way religions are viewed by their members means, of course, that the leaders of religions have to be changing if the religions are to be or to remain representations of the increasingly widening horizon of social unity; if they are to be or to remain meaningful.

But have our religious leaders changed the official stances of our religions enough (or at all) to adapt them to social convergence? Enough to keep them meaningful? While not offered as proof of any kind, the following is food for thought. Reported in Religion in America (Gallup Report 222, March, 1984): 95% believed in God (a name indiating a universal entity, well suited to represent a trans-societal wholity), but only 39% had a "great deal" of confidence in any organized religion. Among teenagers, while belief in God was still 95%; "great deal" of confidence in organized religion was only 25%. The extremely high percentage professing a belief in God in this survey indicates a strong regard for religion itself. This suggests that the negative reaction to organized religions is due to their failure to recognize that the object of religion, the concept of God, represents the trans-societal wholity, a wholity that includes all religions.

In these terms, the insistence by any religion that it is already the one religion (that to which all others must conform) would be as arrogant as it would be futile. For religions to remain (or be) meaningful in our lives they must recognize that they are affected by the move toward unity going on in the world around them. To recognize that their only viable course is their own movement toward unity. (That religions are so affected by societies does not at all mean for Durkheim that religion stands in a kind of secondary or inferior position to society. As the symbolic representation of social solidarity it is the symbol of the meaningfulness of social life.)

Having discussed Cooley and Durkheim, can we see a relationship between the ideas of these theorists? For Durkheim, the viability of societies, that is, the meaningfulness of life in societies once they no longer live in isolation from one another can be maintained only by adopting an openness to one another that's in keeping with feelings of union exchanged between their members. Cooley in his concept of primary ideals also assumes the necessity of such an openness on the part of societies. Both theories involve a movement toward the union of unity, not uniformity. For Durkheim the union involves those from different societies, so uniformity of ways of life cannot be assumed. In Cooley, it is suggested that primary ideals involve the positiveness of care and concern for others, some level of a feeling of unity with others, but not a concern that others become like us. This it seems can be assumed since as standards primary ideals are extended to all; to all necessarily assumes a basic disregard for specific ways in which others may be different from us. Both theorists, it appears, are predicting a movement toward unity (union) based on the extension of positiveness as the orientation of our social nature. That the orientation of our nature enhances the meaningfulness of life.

Simmel

Simmel claims that introspection will produce a view of self as attracted to the positive, as positively oriented, as basically positive. As noted in Chapter Two, this is in keeping with the findings of many of the most well known analysts and more recent experimental research in psychology. But it is also in agreement with a basic belief of religion. All major religions in simply assuming that they will continue in existence can do so only by the further assumption that human beings are attracted to the positiveness that characterizes the transcendent entities that are central to their teaching (God, Nirvana, etc.). That humans, in being attracted to these entities, are themselves positively oriented, basically positive.

Also Simmel's distinction between social and human values implies that the latter are the values that are attractive to all humans, to human nature itself. And his claim that those values include beauty and kindness also matches with the religious ideas of God or Nirvana (a state of Complete Bliss). Indeed, the practice of kindness is an at least official basic teaching of all major religions. While he did not apply his ideas on introspection or social/human values directly to religion, as already indicated, he was interested enough in religion as a social phenomenon to write a book and a lengthy article on it. The following is a very brief presentation of his ideas on the relationship between society and religion.

Simmel describes the basic human condition as characterized by a dissatisfaction with viewing reality as a disconnected variety of things. Rather, that we see them as united in patterns of relatedness; we see them in unities. Even more, that we assume no limit to this unification; we are by nature drawn to seeking higher, more inclusive unities (p. 10). He continues by relating this to religion. A basic characteristic of religion is the experience of the feeling of inclusion in the unlimited union of a "higher order." But, he adds, this feeling is experienced not only in religion but first in a more limited way in areas of secular life. That is, in the positive relations that bind us in union with others. Indeed, for Simmel this experience of union is not only found in our secular life but historically existed prior to and was what gave rise to religion as such (p. 6). Religion is a "spiritual abstraction" from our sensually concrete experiences (p. 4). This process can be seen also as reflected in the acquisition of religious faith on the individual level.

The first experience of all individuals is obviously a secular one. That is, the experience of the infant in the family or surrogate family setting. It is also, typically, a basically positive, happy, satisfying experience. An experience that clearly precedes any religious knowledge and belief that the child may later come to. Since it is central to the teaching of all major religions that there is an Ultimate Entity of positiveness, happiness (Heaven for Judaism, Islam, Christianity; Nirvana for Buddhism, Hinduism), the experience of infants can be seen as a preparation for their later attraction toward, appreciation and acceptance of this teaching. In addition, it provides them with a kind of pre-knowledge of what they will be taught about the Ultimate Entity of their religion. Put another way, the extent to which a young child has not experienced the happiness of the exchange of positive relations would make it more difficult for her or him to believe in the existence of an Ultimate Entity of happiness. (This does not mean that anyone who experienced a lot of unhappiness in childhood cannot believe in such an entity but that it would seem to make it more difficult for her or him to really believe that it is one of kindness.)

Here, like Durkheim, he sees what happens in social relations as affecting religion. Both these theorists can be interpreted as saying that religions grow out of and remain connected to social experience, and, as such, they can, and will, be affected by changes in social experience. In his noting that kindness as a human value is rooted in our nature, Simmel is obviously claiming that our nature is oriented toward the existence of higher unities; his ideas can be seen as coinciding not only with Durkheim's but also with Cooley's idea of the higher unities resulting from the primary ideals.

While Cooley doesn't directly tie his theory to religion as such, his claim that our primary need is only fairly gratified by our primary relations, our strongest experience of union, can be seen as leaving our nature seeking union with something even beyond the feeling of union involved in the extension of the primary ideals to all humanity. Seeking unity with something beyond all human experience.

In short, Simmel is telling us that the rise of religions and, it seems reasonable to assume, their viable maintenance depends directly on the quality of human relations. This idea is far from foreign to any of the world's religions but their efforts should be redirected towards focussing on it if they are to be meaningful agents in our lives. For instance, Christianity might pay much closer attention to the the unmistakable message of the writer of St. John's first letter: One without love can know nothing of God, and again, one who has no love for the sister or brother seen cannot love the God not seen. (Was that early Christian writer a pioneer sociologist of religion?)

Sorokin

In writing of what is required to make life meaningful, Sorokin points to the necessity for an at least adequate satisfaction of our natural needs which are both physical and non-physical (including mental and spiritual). That these needs do not exist independently of one another but, since both are rooted in our nature, they are complementary; indicating that the idealistic culture is the only one that can provide for meaningful life. (Romantic love is a classic example of the complementarity of our needs. Without physical attraction it cannot even begin; without the spiritual dimension, the physical-spiritual attraction, it is not romantic love.)

We have already seen that the "balanced" idealistic (system) culture differs from the others in that the ideational accepts as satisfying, and therefore meaningful, only that which comes from beyond the physical, from beyond the senses; the sensate, only that which comes through the senses, only the physical, material. The sensate, obviously ignoring our non-physical needs, fails also at providing a really satisfying fulfillment of our physical, material needs precisely because its promised rewards are material. Clearly material rewards are quantifiable and things that are quantifiable can be perceived, at any given time, as less than what they might be; as such, less than fully satisfying. Therefore, during the lifetime of any given people the promise of the sensate is that there will be more, life will become even more satisfying; but there will be even more after they're gone. A more satisfying life that they will never enjoy.

But how about the ideational culture? Can emphasizing only the non-material result in the satisfaction of human needs? Even from the standpoint of religions themselves, is this the culture they should be striving to promote, the one in which religion can be most effective?

At first thought, since the ideational like the sensate is so other worldly, so "heavenly," we might be tempted to think so. But we have already seen that religion is very much rooted in our interaction with one another which includes, of course, with the materiality of one another. Is the meaningfulness of life separable from the physical needs and the physical involvement (bodily presence) of people? Can the strong experience of community, so important in the theologies of the Jewish and Christian religions, be attained by neglecting to encourage the bodily as well as the spiritual presence of their members?

No, it seems that like the sensate the ideational culture is far too one- sided to be the basis for meaningful human existence.

Early in its history Christianity seems to have been infected by the gnostic idea that the body was somehow evil. An idea which had the effect of denying the need for bodily presence. Notwithstanding its promotion of marriage and the family it paralleled this with a strong degree of anti-sexual (anti-body) bias. Roman Catholicism continued, at least until the reforms of Vatican Two, to maintain this position. And it can be wondered if its continued refusal to change its rulings on universal clerical celibacy, banning women from the clergy (are they still thought of as temptresses, as dangers to spiritual loftiness?), and artificial birth control (is loving spousal sexual activity ever an evil?) are not related to this position. None of this is intended to mean that Roman Catholic leadership is necessarily consciously motivated by an anti-sexual bias, but to suggest that its tradition (there is no scriptural basis for any of the above) of such a bias could very well be "lingering on."

It would seem logical that the culture best suited for religion would be the idealistic. One in which the meaningfulness of human existence can best be promoted by addressing the material and non-material dimensions of "this world." It would allow not only for proper and appropriate attention to physical as well as spiritual needs but would not suffer from discoveries that challenge the ideational approach.

For example, the idealistic culture allows religion to accept and combine the scientific evidence of physical evolution with the work of a creator directing its development into humanity. This avoids what is a dilemma for religious fundamentalists who while holding for the immediate creation of our species, as we know it, are left with the great problem of explaining the innumerable pre-human fossil finds that indicate progressive development toward modern humanity. (Pure evolutionists have the opposite problem. In insisting that the energy for our evolution was that of physical survival alone, they leave completely unexplained the desire, the wish that Freud himself claims is humanity's most powerful, most urgent one. (Needleman, J., et.al., Religion for a New Generation, 56) The wish for immortality; for survival beyond the physical.)

Durkheim wrote of the convergence of societies and consequently the need for religions to change if they are to stay meaningful. Sorokin also seems to see the meaningfulness of religions dependent on their changing

61

toward the characteristics of the idealistic type society. Both of them can be seen agreeing that it is what happens to society that puts pressure on religion to change. And while Sorokin does not address himself to the value of, the necessity of, positive relations as such, he can be interpreted as doing so in that he saw (p. 314-315) the mistreatment of one another as one of the severe evils of the sensate culture. That relationships between people in this highly rational, calculating culture tend toward power plays involving treating others with anything but kindness or any degree of what Cooley would call primariness. While unlike Cooley he does not suggest that they are rooted in human nature, there would certainly seem to be an agreement between Sorokin and Cooley on the basic necessity of positive relations for meaningful societal life.

Park

Robert Park did not address himself to religion as such. However, as we saw, he was very concerned with the importance for society of its moral order or level, and its relationship to society's political order.

Here I want to expand on the discussion of Park's ideas presented in Chapter 4. There are two reasons for this: to be better able to relate his ideas to (1) Durkheim's prediction for societies in general; and, (2) the general characteristics that religions tend to share as social organizations.

A society with an adequate moral order is one in which its members have a feeling of belonging with one another strong enough that they positively identify with one another as members of their society. In effect, in addition and related to their identification with one another, they have a feeling of belonging to their society itself. Obviously, a less than adequate moral order would mean no society.

The political order is that of formal control; in practice it involves certain members of a society empowered to control at least the public activities and interactions of the members in general.

In a society where the moral order is very strong there is a very strong positive identification of the members with one another and with their society. The strength of such a moral order is evidenced by their high level of care and concern for one another and their society. Such societies are characterized by voluntary cooperation so there is little if any need for a full-time political order; along with the exchange of care and concern all the proper ways of behaving, deeply ingrained in childhood, are readily accepted. Earlier, smaller societies, where everyone knew everyone else were most often of this kind. But, as societies began to grow in size (and complexity) members no longer had personal knowledge of or contact with an increasing number of others of their society, the moral order tended to weaken. As a result not only did an active political order become necessary but it increased in power proportionate to the weakening of the moral order.

As this occurred so did the possibilities for power for the leaders. Power, as we discussed earlier, is most frequently exercised through an increase in laws, in rules and regulations enforced by and on the authority of the political order. Frequently attracted by the opportunity for power (although in some cases the motive may have been the more honorable one of a perceived obligation to preserve the society) the leaders of the political order tended to proliferate the rules and regulations far beyond what the circumstances called for, creating societies characterized by legalism. But regardless of the motivation the imposition of rules and regulations does not seem to be a very effective way to create or maintain peoples' care and concern for or identification with their society. Such qualities are the result of attraction toward, and there is very little that is attractive about rules and regulations.

One way in which political leaders attempt to prevent the loss (or at least severe weakening) of care, concern for and identification with society is by emphasizing to their members the threat of other political orders. (How often have the leaders of the U.S. and the U.S.S.R. attempted - with considerable success - to reinforce allegiance within their respective societies by raising the spectre of the danger from the other.) For a long time, threat from without has been recognized as an effective motive for loyalty within. But it seems to have been much more effective in former times. A growing number of people (especially among the younger and better educated) of an increasing number of societies do not seem to be responding to such threats. The reason for this could be that fear of the political order of others has been replaced by the fear of modern weaponry itself, regardless of who might "fire" first. For this reason it is good to educate the young (especially through films) about the horrors of modern warfare; that it is no longer (if it ever was) the "path to glory" that their elders thought it to be.

It was stated above that as the moral order decreases the political increases. This is the general pattern but an interesting exception can exist. A political order can increase its power on the basis of a strong moral order. The Nazi regime did this by capitalizing on the very strong feeling of loyalty and identification with the fatherland that remained strong despite the temporary chaotic conditions that characterized the German society following World War I. The Japanese leaders were able to do it because their moral order until the end of World War II was so closely allied to their religious feelings of awe for the Emperor and for Japan itself. In both cases extreme chauvinism (a characteristic frequently found where there is a strong moral order) motivated the members of these societies to suffer severely, even die in the cause of expansion through conquest.

In this extension of the ideas of Park a tie-in with Durkheim can be seen, centering on the notion that while too weak a moral order would be chaotic, too strong a one can also be a problem.

For Durkheim a society with a very strong moral order would be one in with which its members have such a powerful feeling of solidarity, identification, that if all societies had such a moral order, his prediction of societal convergence would be meaningless. Social convergence does not involve individuals shifting their identification from their society to another; rather, that societal identification weakens sufficiently to allow for the identification of individuals with other individuals, across societal lines.

In effect his prediction involves networks of individuals (both intra- and extra-societal), as individuals, sharing a feeling of belonging (of identification) at least as strong as their feeling for their respective societies. These networks are flexible entities in that the only requirement for "membership" is individuals liking one another as individuals and, consequently, sharing some degree of care and concern.

This type of social structuring has the beneficial effect of preserving an ongoing sufficient identification of members with their society while allowing for identification beyond it. It would provide a kind of porous social setting in that individuals could easily and quickly pass into new networks, belong to a variety of networks simultaneously and over time. In this way the networks would be linked, giving all individuals, at any given time, a large enough number of positive relationships to provide them with the psychological reinforcement and support (formerly provided by single society membership) our social nature requires.

And what would be the appropriate role of the political orders of the various societies involved in such an arrangement? Their's would be the task of fair taxation to provide for public salaries and public services and the enactment and strict enforcement of a law prohibiting within their boundaries any individuals, groups or organizations from mistreating, suppressing, economically manipulating, generally treating negatively any other individuals, groups, or organizations. Whatever other power the political leaders would have they could not interfere with the guarantees of that law. Moral orders sufficiently strong to preserve each as a society would continue to exist in such societies since such governing would create an atmosphere attractive enough to maintain adequate societal identification by their respective members (as well as the appreciation of visitors).

None of this is to suggest that this ideal condition ever will be reached but that over the long run of history it is at least the direction in which we are moving.

What is the significance of all this for religion? First, it restates a warning we saw in the section on Durkheim: because of social convergence religions had better realize that they too will have to at least match that convergence or wind up with shrinking memberships increasingly comprised of those who reject openness to others. Ironically, memberships characterized by the refusal to follow the tendency of human nature that attracts us toward others as persons, an attraction that goes beyond differences of memberships of any kind. This indeed would be a peculiar position for a religion. Winding up with a membership that in the conviction of its own righteousness would glory in itself as a holy remnant. If the God of any religion had such a remnant in mind it would seem highly unlikely to be one made up of those who reject their natural tendency to love, who refuse to identify with their sisters and brothers in the human family.

The minimal level of convergence that would seem to be required of the religions would begin with a recognition of what they have in common. First, that however they differ in what they believe about or in how they describe The Beyond it is the same Beyond. This is indicated in that The Beyond is in one way or other thought of by all major religions as Absolute Oneness or Union. From the God of Judaism, Islam and Christianity to the Brahman of Hinduism to the Absolute of Buddhism to the Tao of Taoism- in all cases Something that exists beyond all yet somehow embraces all, is in union with all. And there can be only one Absolute Oneness; the different ideas that religions have of it are based on their perception of the manifestations of that Oneness.

Another step, flowing from the above, would be for the various religions to recognize the validity of one another in so far as each recognizes that the Beyond is Absolute Oneness. And to make this clear to their followers.

In light of the recognition of The Beyond as Absolute

Union, much progress could be made if the religions would start defining their ritual practices in ways that would not lead their followers to feel that "in the eyes of the Absolute" they are set apart, separated, from and therefore somehow superior to those of other religions. For instance Christianity could make it clear to its followers that baptism as a ritual does not separate its recipients from anyone enjoying baptism of desire; which by definition is anyone who sincerely seeks after the Absolute Union. Baptism of desire is not a second-class one and it certainly doesn't make those receiving it "honorary or anonymous Christians." It is simply, in Christian terminology, a way of referring to anyone sincerely seeking after the Absolute Union within and through the practices of their own religion or outside any organized religion.

This would in no way reduce the desirability of ritual baptism for Christians. Mainstream Christianity has never defined this ritual as an automatic induction into salvation but rather as an initiation (invitation) into a life demanding love of and service to all (hardly implying that its recipients are set apart or superior to anyone).

As a Christian I would not attempt to illustrate the above idea from the standpoint of other religions. But I imagine that similar adjustments could be made in the explanation of their theological terminology that would correct, if any, ideas that have them consider themselves set apart from, superior to the rest of the human family.

Another step that could be taken by the Christian religions would be to do something about the use of the expression "the Jews" that appears in our scripture. It is generally agreed by all scripture scholars that in all instances involving antagonism this expression is in reference to the Jewish leaders (and certainly not to all of

68

them). What more effective way of reinforcing anti-Semitism than reading such lines as the "the disciples were hiding in fear of the Jews" to a church full of people who take it to mean all the Jews. Since at the time the disciples themselves were still practicing Jews (Acts: going up to the temple for prayers at three-o'clock) to think they were in fear of Jews would be as senseless as writing that Joan of Arc was in fear of the Catholics (although obviously she had much to fear from some Catholics leaders--both securlar and clerical). The language should be changed to read "some of the leaders" or, short of this, that whenever passages containing negative reference to "the Jews" are read the real meaning of it should be clearly explained to the congregations.

Again, as a Christian, my comments are directed toward the use of specifically Christian scripture. If there are any usages of the scriptures of the other religions that could be reinforcing divisions it would be members of those religions that should comment on them.

By promoting the extension of respect and acceptance across religious lines the religions would be promoting in a positive way what the societies would be doing through the enforcement of their law preventing negative behavior within and across societal boundaries. And the benefit derived by the various societies would be enjoyed by the religions. That is, by such a move religions would be promoting our natural tendency (theologically, our God given tendency) to extend positiveness toward all, creating an atmosphere of positiveness that would result in their being more attractive to the growing number of their respective followers who are already positively related to others regardless of their religion.

In this chapter we have looked at the theorists not only

to see what they had to say about and how they could be applied to the phenomenon of religion, but also in order to abstract what they might have in common concerning the conditions necessary for meaningfulness of life. To one degree or another each of them showed concern for relations of positiveness which, because these are relations between individuals as such and not as members of groups, generate movement toward the oneness not of uniformity but of unity. That is, that the logical consequence of such relations is the movement toward a convergence that allows for the retention of self-identify. The completion of this convergence is not a consideration. What is significant is the evidence that it is occurring. And the evidence is there, all we need do is turn our eyes toward it (since it is well known that we tend not to see what we don't look for). To fix our gazes, as so many do, only on the amount of prejudice, discrimination, or negativeness in general that still exists within our societies and between them (and this is a serious problem) logically prevents seeing the change toward positiveness that has been taking place over the long span of historical development. Change not simply toward convergence but one that is increasing at an accelerating rate. Increasing not on a continuous path (which was the mistaken thinking of the champions of the "age of progress") but along an <u>overall</u> advancing route; one the map of which reveals many level places, and some downturns. (For some evidence of this overall advance see again the Durkheim section in Chapter One).

While we applied the theorists to religion, it is important to keep in mind that they are sociologists and, as such, their major concern is with the analysis of society. So whatever suggestions for religions that I drew from them are equally suggestions for society or what goes on between societies. Or, in terms of sociology as a therapeutic medium, suggestions that surely should be taken into account in attempting to aid individuals in finding more meaning in their lives. To implement our understanding of sociology as therapy one of its major concepts, briefly touched on earlier, needs further discussion. That is, the concept of society; a word so commonly used without comment that it seems assumed that everyone understands it to mean the same thing.

But what is society? There are in sociology a variety of ways of defining it, most of which concentrate on it as a system of related structures. A system that coordinates the interactions of its members by conditioning them to its beliefs, its values, its ways in general. Unmistakably, society is such a system.

But in concentrating on this we can give the impression that the behavior of the members of a society cannot be coordinated in harmony, unless they live in compliance to virtually all its ways. While this was a characteristic of the typical earlier society, a noticeable change has been taking place. That is, an increasing number of persons are seeing themselves first as individuals, secondarily as members of their society or of groups within it.

This trend is particularly evident among the younger people of our society and a growing number of others (at least among a larger proportion of younger than older people). This more individual approach to life involves the tendency for noncompliance with at least some of the ways of the society by which they were conditioned. In addition, these individuals, typically, also see others as individuals first, accepting their right to some degree of noncompliance. But it is obvious from what we've discussed that for the survival of any society, which must

71

be characterized by membership that shares at least some level of a feeling of belonging, any noncompliance cannot include persistent patterns of negative behavior.

However, a problem can arise for the members of a society who follow even partially their "own way." While intellectually they accept their freedom to do so they can still be being challenged (somewhere within themselves) by their conditioning to society's "ways." Since the latter are ingrained in us while we're quite young they are not easily disregarded, whether or not we consider them important. It is the damage that can come from this possible conflict with which sociology as therapy is concerned. Even more specifically, when the ways of society are contrary to our natural orientation toward positiveness.

In the following chapter we will look at how the ideas of the theorists can suggest ways in which we may be being conditioned against our nature by the "ways of our society." An attempt to see why our lives may not be as meaningful, as satisfying as they could be. To see, possibly, what we might do as individuals to change our own lives enough to soften if not eliminate any negative affects of society on us. And, if enough of us would do this, would this not have a positive effect on our society itself?

CHAPTER SIX
Sociology As Therapy

While all of them seem to agree on our need for positiveness, what possible light can the approaches of each of the theorists we've covered throw on how our society might be conditioning, affecting, its members in ways contrary to that needed? And what suggestions for lessening or even eliminating these negative affects can be drawn from these theorists?

In tracing the exercise of primary ideals back through the experience of primary relations (where our social nature is formed) to primary needs (with which we are born), Cooley sees the extension of these ideals (extending positiveness to others) as rooted in our nature. Consequently any societal conditioning that tends to prevent our extension of positiveness toward others would be contrary to our nature itself.

With this in mind consider how a highly materialistic and highly competitive society, where individuals are expected (pressured) to succeed on their own, conditions us to concentrate on ourselves and our own material gain. Conditioning us against our nature by tending us to be unconcerned, uncaring about others.

Durkheim concentrated on the needs for solidarity in societal life, seeing this as basic to our nature as social. But then went on to point out that societal life need not be (would not be) confined to one's own society. How, if societies condition their members to restrict their positiveness to "their own," if they condition their members to the idea that friendliness to members of other (or certain other) societies is an act of disloyalty, they are by this not only preventing progress in social convergence but

73

also preventing what is satisfying to, in accordance with our social nature.

An article in the New York Times Magazine (8/10/86) on a camp run for the purpose of bringing harmony between Israel and its neighbors offers evidence for the validity of Durkheim's and Cooley's ideas. Israeli and Arab youngsters (both strongly conditioned by their societies to see each other as "the enemy"), when brought together at the camp for only four days, reported that for the first time they thought of each other as persons. And when parting showed the development of mutual positive feelings since they did so with tears and hugs. Doesn't this tell us something about what their nature (certainly not their societies) tended them toward?

Simmel was concerned with the negative affects on the individual in a society resulting from too much complexity, too much stimulation. Too many detailed demands, too many new situations, new activities, new places, new challenges; in general a way of life that involves a never ending chain of adapting to too much, too fast. We tend psychologically to be more comfortable, more certain with the familiar; since we have experienced it before we are more certain of what it is and how to deal with it. In contrast we are uncertain (or, at least, less certain) when faced with a rapid succession of the new. What Simmel is saying is that a healthy society is balanced between the familiar and the new; warning of the affects of too much of the new too often. He also warned of the possible negative affects of social values on human values (among which is a value on the relaxing atmosphere of kindness). Not only are we experiencing an extreme amount of rapid change but it would seem that we are doing so at least partly as the result of the social value we place on the

74

new, on change itself.

As with Simmel, Sorokin is concerned with balance. His idealistic culture is one of balance. His warning for our present society is that materialism far outweighs the value we tend to place on our spiritual or ascetic dimension. That our society conditions against the pleasure of appreciating, reflecting on ideas for their own sake; against our natural need to enjoy the spiritual feelings of real friendship, real love, which are expressed in commitment to others. Conditions us toward selfishly seeking satisfaction from material pleasures without regard for others (e.g., sex without concern for using, manipulating the other). The strong quest for material satisfaction tends to militate against our natural need for the exchange of positiveness, spiritual experience. Again, the concern here is not directed against the material but the lopsided emphasis on it (materialism) which by its very nature tends to rob us of satisfaction from any other source.

One of the insights gained from Robert Park involves the problems that can arise for individuals in a society characterized by legalism. A condition that frequently indicates a society where positiveness toward others is not very prevalent. Specifically, how are we negatively conditioned by legalism? The law (in addition to the ways it can be misused by a government) tends to be used throughout the citizenry for purposes of manipulation. The age of litigation, rampant suing and countersuing involving sums far in excess of damages, creates a setting of threat to all (with the possible exception of the lawyers). Another problem is that people tend to become selective about the law. Many self-proclaimed champions of "law and order" frequently defy the laws that apply to them, as in the case of illegal strikes or "job actions" by public or private employees. Or, consider the continuous serious damage to our ecology by a number of corporations that break our environmental laws with impunity. Or, the angry and sometimes violent response to being "ticketed" by an increasing number of those who seem to see no reason at all for compliance with parking or even traffic regulations. It should be fairly obvious that the above instances either directly or indirectly inject an attitude into our society that tends to work against our need for positiveness.

What we've discussed so far allows us to distinguish between the sociological and the psychological or psychiatric approaches to therapy. How our emphasis is on looking at what is going on in society itself as the source of individual problems whereas the typical psychological approach concentrates on looking for the source within the individual, including the effects of conditioning by particular others in his or her life. While different the two approaches are really complementary so I am not suggesting that the other approach be in any way replaced by the sociological; but, that in many cases the sources of individual problems cannot be fully gotten at without consideration of societal conditioning. That our problems originate and continue because of particular others (parents, other relatives, teachers, police, or clergy, etc.) is frequently only partly true; partly, because those particular others were also conditioned by our society. If we are counselled that the problem is only with particular others then we have only four choices: resign ourselves to keeping the problem (not a solution, so we'll drop it from our discussion); avoid these people; "stand up to" them in the hope of either "converting" them or "getting them off our backs"; or a more recent trend in psychological therapy, to accept the responsibility for what is going on in one's life. The second and third options tend to keep one almost continuously either "back peddling" or "punching." But the last one if accepted can cause one to see the problem as somehow being her or his own fault in that this can easily be taken to be a message (while maybe not intended by the analyst) that the ways of society are right and therefore should be adapted to. Here, the sociological approach can be a corrective. Through it we can accept responsibility for our behavior by becoming aware that at least many of our problems are not due to our own behavior or to behavior originating with significant others in our lives; after all, as already noted, these others are also part of the same society. Then we can accept responsibility for what we do, not by adapting to society but by shifting our behavior away from full or even any compliance with what we become aware of as societal demands harmful to our nature. In recognizing these demands for what they are non-compliance should not give rise to guilt. What is involved in the sociological approach is rejecting not particular other persons as the cause of the problem (although some of their views may have to be rejected) but damaging conditioning by the society of which both we and these others are members. It is precisely by becoming aware that all or at least many are affected in these negative ways by our society that we should better understand what frequently motivates others who affect us. And, such an understanding can help us accept, not reject them as persons. Psychologically, it is much healthier for us to reject the influence of the damaging demands of impersonal society than to reject other persons. Especially, persons with whom we are emotionally bonded or any persons with whom we are in ongoing contact.

How can we go about rejecting these societal

demands? Simply realizing that they are real causes of many of our problems should invite our closer investigation of them, to see what alternatives we may have. To see if they are really a necessary part of our lives. For instance, is it really necessary for us to accept extreme competition as the only route to success? Can we at least soften considerably the twin affects of fear of failure and fear of others as competitors in the rat-race that is generally promoted by our society? We can come to the realization that we don't have to compete for ever higher slots in our economic world. And, it is very important for our analysis of self through the analysis of society that we realize that this level of competition is precisely what is the general expectation in our society, is what we've been conditioned to by our society. We can come to see that we can see ourselves as successful, contented with our lives, with a reasonably comfortable income. In this way we are being responsible for our behavior without accepting any fault for what might be thought of as being unable (or unwilling) to adapt to society's demands. Indeed, we can feel good about ourselves for being intelligent enough to stay out of the economic "rat race." And, we can do this without rejecting society in general or those with whom we share our lives.

To see the effect on all of us brought on by constant adapting to new experiences could allow us to avoid some of this. Not by retreating to a static existence but beginning by deciding to hold back in some of the areas of change that are not really necessary for us to participate in. Is it really necessary for us to feel pressured into having the "state of the art" models of the many things that our consumer society advertises as vital for our "happiness"? Or, we can make our lives more meaningful by opting for an "activity" that our activity oriented society places no value on at all (probably because it's free): we can take time to "stop (or at least slow down) and smell the flowers" - and we can start by reflecting on, marvelling at, the significance for us of the idea that our nature orients us toward positiveness, friendliness, friendship, love.

CHAPTER SEVEN
Sociology, Psychology, Philosophy, Theology, Physical Science - A Common Thread?

When an idea is commonly arrived at by major representatives of a variety of approaches to the explanation of the nature of reality, wouldn't it suggest a serious consideration of its validity?

It seems that there is such an idea: although expressed variously it is the idea of union or attraction toward union. We'll begin our discussion of it by a further development of Cooley and Durkheim; then move on to a brief look at psychology, philosophy, theology and physical science.

In reflecting on my interpretation of Cooley and Durkheim it becomes obvious that attraction toward union is not only common to but of basic importance to their theories of society.

Cooley's primary relations involve an ongoing actual experience of union with particular others; his primary ideals, an expression of a feeling of union with (concern for) others in general. Likewise, the union and attraction toward wider horizons of union in Durkheim's notion of ongoing friendliness and friendship across societal lines increasingly drawing the world in the direction of a oneness. But here we must be careful to distinguish between the oneness of unity and that of uniformity. Unlike the former the movement toward uniformity would result in the loss of <u>self</u>-identity, all would identify and be identified in terms of their conformity to a uniform way of life.

Cooley clearly had the oneness of unity, not uniformity, in mind since obviously there could be no loss

80

of positive personal identity in the extension of kindness to strangers; or, typically, would there be such a loss between those in primary relations. While he saw that those in primary relations do identify with one another (what Cooley called "mutual identification"), he in no way indicates that this involves the mutual loss of self-identification. Indeed, he states that the primary group is always a "differentiated--unity" characterized by "self-assertion." And, as we've already seen, Durkheim was predicting a feeling of union resulting from the interrelationship of persons, as persons. So he too was writing of some level of friendship, of primary relations.

But Cooley and Durkheim are indicating that what is involved in this is not only the maintenance of positive self-identity but also respect for the right of others to be or remain different. As noted above Cooley's idea of the primary ideal included the extension of concern and even help to total strangers (who remain strangers, identified only as human beings in need of help). Given these circumstances there is obviously no intention (or even any way) of changing the ways of the recipients. And respect for one another's self-identity in primary relations indicates a respect for a differences in selves.

With Durkheim the very idea of forming friendly relations or friendships across the lines of a variety of societies surely assumes that a uniform way of behaving is not expected. (Although logically one area of uniformity would be necessary: the behavioral differences of any participants could not include those that would interfere with the rights of others to be different.) But let's pursue Durkheim a little further on this, expanding on a part of his theory noted in Chapter One.

Central to his first book (<u>The Division of Labor in</u>

Society) are two sequential models of society. (The following is only an overview of Durkheim's presentation of these models.) The earlier society, based on mechanical solidarity, is a one in which all identified as one since they were engaged in the same work activities and, therefore, tended to have identical interests and share in, at least close to, an identical way of life. A model that approximated the oneness of uniformity. The one which would come later is a larger, more complex one which he called a society of organic solidarity. In this model, because the society is larger and more varied in its economic activities, the members would be engaged in different types of work and consequently have somewhat different interests. Because of occupation specialization there is an increase in dependency on one another as suppliers of their varying wants. The mutual feeling of union, despite their differences, is the result of the obvious necessity for their ongoing contact with one another. An experience that most frequently results in friendliness, in some degree of friendship; a sharing of the feeling of belonging together as persons. As a basic need of our nature, the satisfaction derived from this feeling would override, be seen as far more important than the differences among them; resulting in a oneness of unity. In short, the sharing of the feeling of union by persons who are in some ways different suggests that the differences are seen as of little or no importance; that the feeling of union is based on an attraction toward one another that goes beyond their differences to who they are as individuals, as persons (recall our earlier discussion of Simmel's notion of attraction of persons to persons).

If Durkheim believed that this is the developmental direction for any single society it seems reasonable to assume that he had at least something similar in mind when writing of the relationship of individuals to individuals involved in social convergence across the lines of societies. But is Durkheim right? Are we attracted to persons despite our differences? Do the differences no longer matter? Is the transition from societies of mechanical to those of organic solidarity simply another example of social change or does it represent a really radical breakthrough of human relations?

I think he is right and that he is suggesting a radical positive change in human relations.

Isn't it more satisfying to be accepted in friendship (or friendliness) although different in some ways from our friends (or friendly others) than to be accepted (acceptable) only because we are like those others? Aren't we likely to feel, in the latter case, that we are "paying a price" for friendship or friendliness? Don't we have a special appreciation of our friendship (or friendly relations) with those of other nationalities or religious backgrounds precisely because the others are "saying" that it doesn't matter, none of that is important, I like you? Doesn't all this mean a respect for our differences, or respect for our right to be different? Don't we have special appreciation for friendship (or friendly relations) with those of other political persuasions, other interests in general? For those who don't expect us to behave in all the ways they do (again, assuming that our behavior doesn't impinge on their's)? Isn't it more attractive to live in a society where full compliance to others isn't a requirement for acceptance? Where we are not required to forfeit our individuality, our identity? Isn't all this a radical departure from what had been (probably from the start of human history until well into our century)?

83

So far we've been looking at friendship and friendliness as they relate to attraction that crosses lines of societies, an attraction that, at least on the level of mutual positive concern, could connect the world. But let's take a closer look at what that attraction is really toward. In short, that our nature itself tends us beyond our experiences of union with friends and friendly others toward the oneness of unity itself.

To do this we'll restrict the investigation to friendship (though what will be said about it certainly can be applied to romantic love and, although far weaker, to the occasional exchanges of friendliness with acquaintances).

What is a friendship? It's any relationship between two persons characterized by <u>ongoing</u> friendly contact (through physical presence or, when separated, through communication) indicating some degree of a feeling of union, of belonging together. As such, it is the same phenomenon whether it involves family members (while some of these involve love it is typically not of the intensity of romantic love) or those outside the family; this is why Cooley included both in the primary group. But a feeling of union, of belonging is a feeling of connectedness.

Friendship involves a feeling experienced <u>within</u> individual friends because of what <u>connects</u> them, what exists between them. And, it is one of the most powerful forces in our lives. Our total reality <u>as persons</u> (personalities) was generated by what existed (what went on) <u>between</u> us and the other members of our initial primary group. The positive <u>within</u> feeling we have for the others of that group began when and because they reached out to us fulfilling our primary need for positiveness.

But, could our primary need have been met by other than those particular persons who did, in fact, meet it? Of

84

course; any others who might have reached out with the positiveness of care, concern, affection would have met our primary need. What was important for us is that some others did reach out, did connect with us. (Obviously, I am not at all suggesting that those who actually did connect with us are no more important to us than any others who might have.)

Our experience in later childhood and as adults provides us with an even clearer illustration of this notion that it is the connectedness itself that is so important. The most obvious thing to each of us is that as we progress through life our need for primary relations continues to be met not only by our initial primary group but also by a series of others. We had friends in early grade school years at least some of whom we no longer even recall but, at that time, they were part of our network of people who were our primary relations. Now there are most likely people in our network of primary relations whom we didn't even know a year or so ago. The personnel seems to be interchangeable. As noted regarding our initial primary group, this is not the say that our current friends are not important to us as individuals, they most assuredly are. The point is that as we "lose" some we "gain" others. In short, the continued fulfillment of you and me as persons does not depend on our relationship with any specific, particular others. It is the relationship itself (what exists between them) that satisfies the mutual needs of friends. Again, friendship always involves a reaching out. Friends reach out to each other, extend beyond themselves as individuals. In a real sense friendship is exchanged in "mid-air" and it is through the connecting (connectedness) that the mutual needs are met; through that connecting that the mutual within feelings of friendship are created

85

and maintained.

Can a very simple experiment provide evidence of this? Think right now of one of your friendships. Consider if it is not the mutual recognition by you and your friend that you care for, like one another <u>as special persons</u> that is the basis of and maintains the within feeling of friendship you both experience. Consider further that the within feelings of friendship began only after (but immediately after) that recognition was mutual. A caring for one another as special persons that is communicated sometimes consciously but more often subconsciously through subtle signals. For instance, spontaneous smiles <u>exchanged between</u> friends when reunited even after a brief separation; signals sent out, without conscious decision, that "say" it's good to be with you again. As <u>exchanged</u>, these signals are sent and received <u>between</u> the friends (physically as well as mentally since what are received are images of light traveling from and to the faces of each). As <u>between</u>, these signals are what connect individuals as friends. And this connectedness is a reality independent of the within feeling of friendship of each of the friends since signals of liking each other had to be mutually recognized (connected, exchanged) prior to the existence of the within feelings (indeed, it is what causes them); and, this connectedness must be continued if these feelings are to be maintained. There is an understandable difficulty with our accepting the reality of this connectedness since we experience only its affects, <u>our own</u> within feeling. We have a strong tendency to think of ourselves as self-developed, of our total reality as somehow self-activated and encased within us. A tendency that is a negative by-product of individuality blinding us to the fact that without the reality of the connectedness between ourselves and others, from earliest infancy, we would have no concept of self at all.

It is the reality of the relationship itself that forms and maintains us as persons. As we form new friendships, as we do so frequently in our highly spatially mobile society, it is the friendship relationship itself toward which we are attracted. But friendships are not formed by pure accident. Before two people can become friends each has to be predisposed to attraction to positiveness outside her or himself. Only this would make it possible for each of them to become attracted to some positive characteristics in the other. [Erich Fromm, whose university education was in sociology, indicates that these positive characteristics are basically human ones. That we are attracted toward others in so far as they exhibit "essentially human qualities." (p. 135.) To be attracted toward means to be extended beyond oneself as an individual, and mutual attraction toward means extension beyond and, therefore, between both selves. As such it connects the selves; the feeling of union we experience within is in a real sense caused by a connection between ourselves and others.

Connectedness or oneness for sociology, then, is in the positiveness of relationships; in the positiveness, of friendship (and, of course, of love). Without the predominance of exchanged positiveness society itself, by definition a unity, could not exist. As such, while in all probability one will never exist, a perfect society, based on positive exchanges only, is at least a logical possibility. A society based on negative exchanges only (or even the predominance of them) is not. Conflict as a form of negativeness can and has been at times a corrective to social problems. But as a corrective it is valuable only in so far as it corrects. Correcting a societal problem has the affect of moving society toward increasing positiveness. (Karl Marx certainly recognized this in his observation that the ultimate goal of revolution is a peaceful world.)

For sociology the movement toward unity, union, oneness is based on the attraction of human nature toward positiveness, toward positive rather than negative behavior. A very sound basis since it is obvious that, while they may engage in it, virtually all people resent being the recipients of negative behavior. Only masochists appreciate the behavior of sadists; and neither are considered by mental health professionals as typical representatives of humanity. Even the religious command to extend love to one's enemies doesn't mean loving their negativeness but overlooking it (with the hope that the attractiveness of the positiveness shown toward them will result in their reciprocation).

While our cultures can certainly condition us otherwise, there is nothing in our nature that would prevent the movement toward positiveness. Cooley states this in his model of primariness; that since our natural primary need is met by our primary relations in only a "fairly satisfactory" manner we are tended toward adding to that satisfaction through the primary ideals. Durkheim can be seen as also agreeing, especially by his emphasis on the need for social solidarity required by our social nature. Incidentally, Charles Darwin also recognized this in stating that only artificial (i.e., not natural) barriers can prevent our "social instinct" of "sympathy" from extending to every race and nation (p. 100). Through our nature, then, we would be increasing in the direction of oneness; increasing our connectedness through the attraction of friendliness and friendship. And, since societies can change but nature does not, it is suggested that ultimately our nature will prevail, will succeed as a corrective to societal conditions that limit our attraction toward others in general. The increase in social contact between individuals of different societies, increase in the knowledge of other ways of doing things, tends to result in the weakening of the power of their own societies to condition their behavior. This is so not necessarily because the "other ways" are seen as better but that what is learned is that there are other ways. When people know of only one way of behaving they are completely conditioned to that way.

Let's now continue our journey with oneness by at least peeking through the windows of psychology, philosophy, theology and physical science.

There is a relatively new branch of psychology (referred to earlier) that has conducted a number of experiments suggested that human beings are oriented toward altruistic behavior. That not only are we prone to helping others but, as some of the experiments indicate, we take pleasure in making others happy. And, apparently any others since in the experiments the recipients of the altruistic acts are strangers to those performing them. (A good source for a description of these experiments, also cited in Chapter 5, is Daniel Bar-Tal's book, Prosocial Behavior.) Certainly such positiveness extended toward others can be seen as related to our theme of attraction toward oneness. And, if it is argued that since there is a reward to self (a feeling of self-satisfaction, of pleasure) that selfishness, not altruism, is involved, then it certainly is a very beneficial selfishness in that everyone benefits from it.

In terms of the relationship between our nature and positiveness, it seems that we are benefitted even by simply observing the extension of positive behavior. David

McClelland, a Harvard psychologist, has been repeating an experiment (reported in <u>OMNI</u> magazine, October, 1987) revealing that an antibody for preventing colds and flu is increased (and remains so for about an hour) by watching a film depicting the tender caring (positiveness) of Mother Teresa for lepers and dying children. And this increase takes place even in those subjects (about half of the total) who are depressed by the vivid portrayal of the afflicted or who have a negative view of Mother Teresa herself because of her stance against abortion. McClelland concludes (very logically, it would seem) that since in those cases it is not love for Mother Teresa then this affect on the immune system must be in response to the altruistic acts, the love, positiveness she is extending others. It seems that simply reflecting on the extension of love, on oneness with others, favorably affects even our physical nature.

Many major philosophies and theologians address themselves to the notion of the connectedness of reality. Some will describe this with expressions such as the "ground of being" (<u>the</u> existent that underlines and, therefore, connects all reality). Or, as the complete "world of ideas" to which all things are connected in that the reality of the physical world is only relative; that it is only a reflection of the absolute reality of the archetypical ideas in the world beyond. Or, as the prime mover, the unmoved mover that relates all things. Or, simply as God, or some other Supreme Entity from which all came and to which they will return.

But that philosophers and theologians make a claim for such a connectedness isn't very noteworthy since this has been a concern of these disciplines since they have been in existence. But our commonly held view is that science deals only with the real observable world, so such talk would be heresy for scientists. This is because the average person outside of science (and even some who work at science) knows little if anything about the implications of the new physics for ideas of the connectedness, the oneness of at least all physical reality.

I am not going into the details of the amazing claims of coming from this approach to science simply because I understand so very little about them. But on a level beyond these details at least two radically new ideas are definitely being seriously discussed in the house of science. One, the recognition of the profound mystery of the reality which it is striving to explain; and, two, that such striving is toward "uncovering" a phenomenon that would be, in itself, the unifier of all reality.

First let us look to several monumental scientific figures for their views of the mystery, the elusiveness of what they are seeking. (I am indebted to Gary Zukav, The Dancing Wu Li Masters, for pointing out all but Oppenheimer.)

Max Planck, generally acknowledged as the founder of quantum physics, wrote in his the Philosophy of Physics, that what science is seeking will ultimately never be rationally explainable but may be understood only through "poetic intuition.:" (p. 83).

Werner Heisenberg states in his Physics and Philosophy, that we don't and never will observe reality in itself. (p. 58).

Niels Bohr in Atomic Theory and Human Knowledge states that quantum mechanics entails not only a rejection of the classical scientific method that presumed that physical reality could be disclosed with certainty but that physical reality itself must be thought of in a totally new

91

way. (p. 60).

J. Robert Oppenheimer in <u>Uncommon Sense</u> claims that the "ways of thinking" about that for which we have evidence and those of eternity are complementary, neither alone reveal all of reality. (p. 53).

That the above statements concern mystery that will forever remain beyond the understanding of science needs no further comment.

Regarding the second part, that the strivings of science are toward an explanation that would be <u>in itself</u> the unifier of all reality, let's consider the basic implication of what scientists call GUT or Grand Unifying Theories. In the February 5, 1983 issue of <u>Science News</u>, Dietrick Thomsen, Senior Editor/Physical Sciences, states that for a long time now physicists have been dissatisfied with the notion ofthe universe being controlled by four separate forces of nature and consequently have been looking for a theory that would show them to be different manifestations of a "fundamental underlying unity." (Interestingly David Bohm, a British physics, refers to this as "That-which-is." (Zukav, p. 323) Is this not suggestive of the theological "ground of being" or the Biblical "I am Who Am"?)

Logically, why would the physicists be looking for this "fundamental underlying unity"? A grand dream spun simply from baseless speculation? Scientists don't like being thought of as so frivolous. It seems that their observation of the unity of localized existence attracts them to the conviction that all of existence is a unity; and that as a unity it should not be the result of separate forces but of one force detected in several forms.

The importance of what I am getting at doesn't involve <u>what</u> the scientists are doing to discover the unifying force (I already told of my widespread ignorance of that) or whether they ever demonstrate its existence, but that they seem convinced that it does exist.

Our concern with the oneness of unity seems to be shared by the scientists; a basic connector of the vast variety of things in nature. A connection that while uniting them does not reduce them to a uniformity.

Psychologists, theologians and scientists, while using different labels, seem to be interested in oneness. Seem to be convinced that somehow it is involved in nature. Sociologists (like the psychologists), of course, are not concerned with a unifier of all reality. But as we saw, especially with Cooley and Durkheim, they are concerned with the unifying force of the mutual attraction of friendliness (positiveness); the force unifying not only a society but societies. Cooley's concentration on primariness leaves no doubt of this and neither does Durkheim's concern with positiveness as that which is attracting individuals across societal lines into a new form of solidarity. Both are concerned with the unifier of all social reality. Primariness and Solidarity are union, connectedness, oneness; and, are possible only through mutual positiveness or attraction.

Moreover, Durkheim writes of the ideal (the symbolic idea) of the perfect "society," the fullness of the feeling of solidarity. This he suggests would be approached increasingly by the natural attraction of a social life of a "new sort," a wholity resulting from the feeling of union exchanged between individuals within and across societal lines. In short, he claims that the idea of an ideal society comes from nowhere else but the experience (at any given time) of social life (1965, p. 470); that it is rooted in the basic human condition, in our social nature. Since it is our nature that attracts us toward union we will be attracted

93

toward it wherever the opportunity for it presents itself. As we saw in Chapter One he specifies why he believes that this attraction ultimately extends across societal lines. (And, as we noted later, in this he appears close to Simmel's thinking on the attraction of persons to persons.)

When a society reaches occupation specialization to the degree that its members no longer feel a union based on common jobs (with their common interests) the one bond they see uniting them is their common humanity. And quite obviously such a bond, by definition, would be universal, existing between all humans within and across all societal lines. In the same place he states that the value on the human person takes on "a religious nature." And since he sees religion (as symbolic) as that which transforms social experience to an ideal, to perfection, he is suggesting that the new wholity, encompassing both intra- and inter-societal positive contacts of union, will increasingly assume the status of the ideal.

Isn't the obviously increasing concern with human rights, in an increasing number of areas of the world, an indication of our growing perceived bond of common humanity? Can't this concern be seen as a indicating an emerging attraction toward the concept of common humanity as the ideal?

The ideal, the perfect; what better words to connote positiveness. Our social nature itself tending us toward the idea of perfect solidarity, perfect oneness, perfect positiveness. Can Cooley and Durkheim be seen as concerned with less than the unifier of all social reality? Concerned with less than the energy of mutual positiveness and attraction as the only one that can produce social solidarity; the only energy with the potential or power to effect the oneness of unity? In addition to all its

94

worthwhile endeavors, including the great number of them concerned with the negative, can't sociology, today, be at least somewhat concerned with the affects of positiveness? If not it stands apart from its own founder, August Comte, who wrote of his firm conviction that the direction in which humanity is progressing is being guided increasingly by our "noblest tendencies." (Simpson, 53).

Social behavior is predominantly positive behavior. Today that positiveness is no longer restricted to the within of relatively isolated societies. Today societies can abe seen as converging; increasingly, positiveness is reaching beyond what had been the solid walls of nations, regions and local communities, of ethnicity and religion. Through social convergence, societies are converging toward a oneness of unity. This is a phenomenon to which more attention must be given, more investigation of it must be conducted; sociology (for Comte, Durkheim, Cooley, Simmel, etc.) is not merely the science of societies but of society itself. Society itself, especially now, is what is emerging from the convergence of societies. Society is the growing awareness of the ever widening sphere of solidarity. For Durkheim the consciousness of consciousnesses is no longer a reference only to a society but to a world of converging societies.

Sociology is a science and science is an ongoing process restricted only by its methodology; that is, careful, objective analysis of whatever is observable, conducted in the light of theoretical generalization. But, so many sociologists have reduced methodology to method, to one method. Limited it to research that involves high-level statistical analysis of quantifiable data as the only valid endeavor of sociology; and, unfortunately, the computer, despite all its virtues, seems to be encouraging this tendency. In addition, so many American sociologists have limited their interests to neutral and negative or problem areas of human behavior, seemingly seeing no importance in the positive. Such arbitrary restrictions have tended to severely limit the effectiveness of sociology itself. Have tended to exclude from the limits of its vision areas of human behavior that are not only obviously there waiting to be observed but areas that could provide us with a more optimistic view of our future.

Such limitations were not what Durkheim envisioned. He clearly states that while we do not know how far the explanations of sociology may go, no pre-established limitations on them can (or should) be set. (1965, p. 495-496).

Nor were they in the vision that Comte had for his infant sociology. For him it was the function of sociology to involve itself in all important areas of speculation in order to bring them "into unity." (Simpson, 134).

Finally, an irony in sociology's neglect of positive behavior that involves the very name of our discipline. The word sociology means the study of companions (socii) and the word companions means those who share bread (panis) with one another.

POSTSCRIPT

The way of life (the culture) of any society is a wholity involving an interrelationship of all its "parts" (political, economic, scientific, religious, etc.) including the ideas promoted by them. As such, these "parts affect one another; supporting or opposing one another depending on the degree of correspondence of their ideas. In light of this I want to expand on our discussion of the recent ideas of psychology and physical science; to look at the ideas of these "parts" of society as interrelated with those of religion, to see if they support or oppose those of religion.

Before continuing two things should be made clear. First, theories about what is not observable as well as what is observable are never provable (recall Planck, Heisenberg, and Bohr). They are beliefs about reality and are believable to the degree that they are reasonable. The reasonableness of any belief is the most support we can ever have for it; and the more support for it, the more reasonable it is. Second, support from one "part" for the reasonableness of the ideas of another "part" of society is not at all necessarily intended. That is, it does not necessarily mean agreement with the ideas themselves.

Evidence from psychology and physical science for or against the reasonableness of religious ideas would be very significant since, like religion, these are the only generally recognized fields that make claims concerning such mysteries as the reality, the origin, and the destiny of humanity, and of the universe itself. And it is also very significant that, unlike those of religion, these claims or speculations, while not proven by, are frequently based on some level of experimental evidence.

William James, probably the most eminent American

psychologist, writes of the potential of the human mind to consciously sense that a "part" of us is in union with something (a "MORE") that extends indefinitely beyond our conscious state (p. 508). That a dimension of our reality is in union with something that exists completely beyond the world of our conscious knowledge (p. 515). Lewis Thomas, president emeritus of Sloan Kettering Institute, supports James' claim in citing the results of experiments that give evidence that our unconscious has medical knowledge that is consciously unknown to the world' most learned physicians (p. 64).

Albert Einstein's famous formula ($E=Mc2$) indicates that all observable things are simultaneously matter and non-matter. Indeed, that what we call matter is in reality compacted non-matter (energy); and that when material things as such are destroyed their reality continues on in the form of non-matter (unfortunately, well illustrated by the resulting reality of the matter in an atom bomb).

In each of the above there was no intention of reinforcing the religious belief in an all knowing divine entity that exists beyond our conscious experience, yet is in union with us; or that when our bodies cease to exist a non-material "part" of us continues on. But they can be seen as ideas parallel to and, as such, support for the reasonableness of those religious beliefs.

Science in general now believes that the universe as we know it had a beginning, that it originated from nothing or virtually nothing. And we've already noted that scientists also believe that the several forces of nature known today are manifestations of one unifying force that has been shaping the universe from its beginning. But is all this due to chance?

At least several well established scientists claim that

chance alone could not account for our universe and all it contains (including life and consciousness) developing from virtually nothing.

Paul Davies, chair of theoretical physicist, Newcastle upon Tyne, England, states that evidence that the universe resulted from design is "overwhelming" (1989, p. 203). Brandon Carter, Cambridge Astrophysicist, expressing the same idea, states that if in the early stages of the formation of the universe the force of gravity had been stronger or weaker by no more than 1 over 10 followed by 39 zeros, no stars (suns) could have been formed (Talbot, p. 195). Davies also claims that life on Earth generated purely by chance is "ludicrously impossible" (1989, p. 118). Fred Hoyle, founder of the Cambridge Institute of Theoretical Astronomy, reinforces this with his claim that the odds of such a happening would be 10 followed by 39,999 zeros to 1 (Talbot, 195).

These scientists are in no way claiming the involvement of a divinity, a God. Davies rejects pure chance in favor of an increasing complexity of physical laws; Hoyle refers to a hierarchy of intelligences, topped by the universe itself as intelligent. However, accepting the idea of one unifying force that fashioned the universe and rejecting the idea of pure chance can be seen as allowing for the reasonableness of belief in a divine designer. This is significant since it was science that first challenged religious beliefs. It was science, before Planck and others, that claimed on the assumed certainty of its "proven" ideas that all religious beliefs were superstitious nonsense, scientifically unreasonable.

Actually science and religion, as Durkheim noted (1965, 479), are complementary and the leaders of each would do well to recognize this. The province of science is the explanation of physical nature, including the conditions under which our universe came into existence, by what laws it developed, how it will end. In short, to uncover as much as possible about the laws of nature, how nature works. This monumental and magnificent task is in no way hindered by a belief that an intelligence (a God) designed it all. Science, investigating the totality of nature, stands on its own, independent of where nature and its laws came from, independent of the God question.

The province of religion is the explanation of humanity: our relationship to the totality of nature, to God and one another, our ultimate destiny. None of which depends on any discoveries within the province of science, on any scientific demonstrations of how nature works. (Indeed, religions have never claimed that their scriptures, on which they base their beliefs, are scientific treatises.) It is of no advantage to religion to challenge the demonstrated workings of nature (and very frequently results in embarrassment--consider the Galileo and Scopes incidents). Equally, it is of no advantage to science to attempt to demonstrate, as John Gribben does (p. 392), that the origin of nature had no need of a God. After discussing the theory that Stephen Hawking presented in 1981 on the origin of the universe, Gribben claims it to be not only a good scientific explanation that involves no need for a God but that it reduces all other ideas of the origin of the universe "into insignificance." There are two problems with Gribben's claim. First, it is only logical to assume that nothing less than proof of an idea would be required for it to reduce all competing ideas to no significance. But scientific theories are no more provable than those of religion. Max Planck (even more directly than in his earlier statement) leaves no doubt of this in claiming that what scientists know of reality are measurements of it, but measurements provide "no direct information about... reality." Therefore, theories of reality can "never logically" be demonstrated to be true (1959, p. 43). And Hawking himself very unambiguously states that "theories can't be proved" (p. 167). Second, Hawking doesn't seem to concur with Gribben that his theory eliminates the need for a God. In John Boslough's book, Stephen Hawking's Universe, published four years after 1981, Hawking is cited as claiming "clearly religious implications" in any discussion of "the origin of the universe" (p. 109). Whatever Dr. Hawkings' belief is concerning the existence of a God, and this is clearly his own business, his claim certainly doesn't detract from the reasonableness of an affirmative one.

If the fundamentalists of religion and science would retrieve their minds from the nineteenth century (or earlier), would stop seeing one another as the enemy, they would see that their respective tasks are not a danger to one another. That, in light of the increasing parallels in their ideas, they can even be truly complementary.

Perhaps the most significant area of complementarity of science and religion goes beyond parallels of specific ideas about reality. Perhaps it is that the basic message of non-fundamentalist scientists and religionists is that the totality of reality is more than we are capable of knowing.

Finally, the leaders of the world religions should see their own complementarity in their common belief that there is an absolute entity existing beyond all human experience that is related in a positive way to all humanity; that as such, even when called by different names, it is the same entity that they profess. To see that the real threat to religion is not secularization but the scandal to "the world" of the often bitter divisions in humanity cause by the explicit or implicit claims of religions that the others are in error. Claims that at least imply a certainty of knowledge of what is by definition beyond all human experience and, as such, beyond the certainty of human knowledge. In short to see that ironically the real enemy of religion has been religions themselves.

But this seems at least beginning to change, a change not unrelated to increasing social convergence. Ecumenical dialogue is beginning, if only slowly; mutual recognition of validity, at least in principle, is under way. And, considering the history of religious relations, this in itself is a significant breakthrough. And shouldn't the progress of this movement be furthered by the growing complementarily between science and religion. And lastly, shouldn't it be furthered since it would fulfill two basic yearnings of "the human heart": to be in positiveness with all, to be free of the anxiety of antagonisms; and to be united with what truly would be the Absolute Entity.

REFERENCES

Alba, R., "The Twilight of Ethnicity Among American Catholics", in Majority and Minority, ED. N. Yetman, 4th Ed, Allyn and Bacon, Boston, 1985.

Barnett, L., The Universe and Dr. Einstein, N.Y., Bantam Books, 1957.

Bar-Tal, D., Prosocial Behavior, N.Y., Halsted Press, 1976.

Bohr, N., Atomic Theory and Human Knowledge, N.Y., J. Wiley, 1958.

Boslough, J., Stephen Hawking's Universe, N.Y., Avon Books, 1989.

Cooley, C.H., Social Organization, N.Y., Schocken Books, 1962.

Darwin, C. The Descent of Man, Princeton, N.J., Princeton University Press, 1981.

Davies, P., The Cosmic Blueprint, N.Y., Simon and Schuster, 1989.

Durkheim, E., Suicide, N.Y., Free Press, 1951.

_____, The Elementary Forms of Religious Life, N.Y., Free Press, 1965.

Freud, S., The Future of An Illusion, N.Y., Liveright Publishing Co., 1955.

Fromm, E., Escape From Freedom, N.Y., Discus Books, 1968.

Gallup, G., Religion in America, Princeton, N.J., Gallup Report (222), 1984.

Glasser, W., The Identity Society, N.Y., Harper and Row, 1975.

Gribben J., In Search of the Big Bang, N.Y., Bantam Books, 1986.

Hawking, S., <u>A Brief History of Time</u>, N.Y., Bantam Books, 1988.

Heisenberg, W., <u>Physics and Philosophy</u>, N.Y., Harper and Row, 1958.

Mumford, L., <u>The City in History</u>, N.Y., Harcourt, Brace and World, 1961.

Needleman, J., et al., <u>Religion for a New Generation</u>, N.Y., Macmillan, 1977.

Oppenheimer, J., <u>Uncommon Sense</u>, Boston, Birkhauser, 1984.

Park, R., "Human Ecology", <u>American Journal of Sociology</u>, July, 1936.

Planck, M., <u>The Philosophy of Physics</u>, N.Y., Norton, 1936.

_____, <u>The New Science</u>, N.Y., Meridian Books, 1959.

Simpson, G., <u>August Comte</u>, N.Y., T.Y. Crowell, 1969.

Sorokin, P., <u>The Crisis of Our Age</u>, N.Y., E.P. Dutton, 1941.

Talbot, M., <u>Beyond the Quantum</u>, N.Y., Bantam Books, 1988.

Thomas L., <u>The Medusa and the Snail</u>, N.Y., Viking Press, 1979.

Wolff, K., <u>The Sociology of Georg Simmel</u>, N.Y., The Free Press, 1950.

Yankelovich, D., <u>The New Morality</u>, N.Y., McGraw-Hill, 1974.

Zukav, G., <u>The Dancing Wu Li Masters</u>, N.Y., Wm. Morrow, 1979.

ABOUT THE AUTHOR

A veteran of World War Two, Dr. McGarry was engaged in a variety of activities — from office work to building houses — before settling on an academic career. He received a Ph.D. in sociology from Fordham University and has been at Villanova University since 1963.

DATE DUE

HIGHSMITH 45-220